Fumbling Towards Freedom

Initiations on the path of Awakening

Rajyo Allen

Manor House

Cataloguing in Publication Information:

Title: Fumbling Towards Freedom / Rajyo Allen
Names: Allen, Rajyo, author.
Description: Contents/subtitle: Initiations on the path of Awakening

ISBN 978-1-988058-96-2 (softcover)
ISBN 978-1-988058-97-9 (hardcover)
Also available in digital form via Kindle ebook

BISAC: BIO023000; BIO026000; OCC019000; OCC010000; OCC011000; SEL016000; SEL032000;

First Edition
Front cover photo: Dmitry Molchanov / Shutterstock
Cover Design-layout / Interior- layout: Michael Davie
Edited by Susan Crossman, Crossman Communications
Proof-read by Theo Lovett
240 pages / 67,340 words. All rights reserved.

Published October, 2022 / Copyright 2022
Manor House Publishing Inc.
452 Cottingham Crescent, Ancaster, ON, L9G 3V6
www.manor-house-publishing.com (905) 648-4797

For my father, who was everything to me.
And for my little girl, who did the best she could.
And for all the little boys and girls
struggling to find their way in this world,
through tragedy and trauma.

Acknowledgements

I would like to acknowledge all the people that have been so much part of my journey and of shaping who I am, and for all the support I have received in bringing this book to completion.

My thanks to Julia Petrisor for her invaluable support in helping me to shape my story into something of a timeline.

To Susan Crossman, my editor, for being solidly by my side, as cheerleader and guide, for supporting and encouraging me through all the challenging places, and for her absolute and sincere belief that my story needs to be told.

To Subhuti, my friend and fellow traveler in Osho's world, for all his brilliant editorial skills in cutting away the dross to help bring the jewels of my journey into the forefront.

To Theo Lovett, who stepped in at the last minute and saved us from many typos and grammatical errors with his brilliant proof reading skills.

To Michael Davie and Manor House, for believing in me, and saying "Yes!" to publishing this book

To my beloved husband Vinit, for seeing me and loving me always, unconditionally. Your love, devotion, patience, acceptance, humility and humor are my place to come home to when I'm weary of the world and all its woes. Thank you for making a safe place for me to be, for bringing magic and beauty into my life and for being my friend and partner on the path of Love and Freedom.

To Alima, my lifelong friend and spiritual companion, for your absolute unwavering commitment to the Truth, amidst all the messiness of life. You have been my witness through it all, and I don't think I could have done it without your unconditional love and support throughout.

To Britta, my friend and colleague on this journey of healing and transformation, through twenty years of leading workshops together, through all the grace and grit. I am grateful for all the ways we have grown, and our hearts been opened by fierce and tender love.

To Paritosh, for being the wild and crazy sister that began the work of facilitating deep transformation in groups with me. To Gina, Debbie, Pravasi, Julie and Ruth, who continue to lead the workshops in the UK, for all your love and devotion and wicked sense of humor that sheds so much light in the world.

To Mary O, my friend and business coach, thank you for seeing me, and supporting me to write this book and for helping me step into the next, and the next evolution of my journey.

To all my dear friends, too many to mention; you know who you are, who have seen me when I could not see myself, and helped me remember that I am, as we all are, so much more than we know ourselves to be.

To my father, for being my friend on the path of awakening. What a gift you gave me to share this love of Truth. It was your example that inspired me to begin to lead workshops and to write. I follow in your footsteps. You are in my heart always and everything I do is in your name.

To my brother, Gray. You inspire me with your dedication to your creativity and your music, your care for your community and your commitment to standing up against injustice to help bring about a better world for all. You are a giant in my eyes.

To my spiritual friend and teacher Miranda, for your guidance and support and the example and inspiration you showed me to let go, be nothing, do nothing and let Grace lead the way.

To Osho, my beloved Master, for giving me a hunger for Freedom, and the most incredible worldwide community of lovers and friends. For the gift of sitting in your presence for so many years and the fragrance of Zorba the Buddha you brought into the world. For giving me the unshakable experience of living in a world where Love is the overarching abiding Truth,

Silence is the doorway to that Truth and we celebrate all of the beauty and sorrow in this wondrous holy dance of Life. My deepest bow of gratitude, always.

To the MeToo Movement for opening up the conversation around abuse of women. I wish to acknowledge some material that may be difficult for some to read, knowing that there were instances in my life which could be perceived as abuse. Although that was not my experience, I understand that this was often normalized in those times.

For those whose lives may have been affected by similar experiences, my deepest wish is for healing from the trauma for all.

About the Author

After witnessing her mother's sudden death when she was just five years old, Rajyo went on a personal journey to heal from that trauma and find her true purpose.

Following a youth spent as a free spirit indulging in alcohol, drugs, and sex, Rajyo's journey led her to Osho's ashram in India, where she spent several years, and discovered a lifelong yearning for spiritual awakening. Along the way, she received training in areas of spiritual and psychological healing, counseling and group facilitation.

After leaving the ashram, Rajyo was inspired to develop innovative and transformational Rites of Passage workshops. After 25 years of presenting her programs while living in Europe and the U.S., Rajyo and her husband moved to Asheville, North Carolina, to create and run a transformational retreat center Samasati Sanctuary (https://samasatisanctuary.org).

Rajyo is a spiritual teacher and soul mentor. Her depth of experience as both a student and teacher in the psycho-spiritual world enables her to offer a rich blend of tools to bring a uniquely transformative experience.

She is also a certified spiritual life coach, counselor, somatic trauma healer and has been a yoga, meditation and mindfulness teacher for over two decades.

Rajyo's current work is based on the Alchemy of Awakening (https://alchemyofawakening.net) which helps people awaken to a deeper level of soulfulness and spiritual maturity in this pivotal time in history. Her deep passion is to help people live a more embodied, heart-centered and authentic life and bring back a sense of the sacred to our world.

Fumbling towards Freedom is her first book.

Praise for *Fumbling Towards Freedom*

Rajyo's racy account of her life's journey on the path to spiritual awakening is raw, real, honest and vulnerable. Recommended!

Deva Premal (Grammy-nominated musician)

This delightful story about the trials and tribulations of the spiritual journey reflects the struggles we all endure as we turn the slings and arrows of our destiny into wings of freedom. Blending spiritual insight with a fascinating tale, the author shows how the journey to enlightenment, peace, and freedom is never a straight line. You will laugh and cry, but in the end this tale will remind you that whether in darkness or light, grace is always present.

Anodea Judith, Ph.D., author, *Eastern Body, Western Mind; Wheels of Life;* and *Waking the Global Heart*

Fumbling towards Freedom is a beloved companion for anyone sincerely wanting to navigate the promises and perils of a non-traditional path home. Rajyo writes with refreshing candor and honesty about the precious wisdom we can only retrieve from skinning our knees. This book is a gem.

Miranda Macpherson, author, *The Way of Grace*

A personal story about the author's rites of passage that has special relevance at this time when our entire species — our entire planet — enters a new rite of passage.

John Perkins, author, *Confessions of an Economic Hitman* and *Touching the Jaguar*

Rajyo has led a fascinating life, traveling the globe in search of spiritual awakening. In this book, she provides very honest and vulnerable insights about the challenges of such a life. She shares highs and lows, including a battle with cancer and death of beloveds with her profound devotion to a challenging path and her longing for true freedom. It's a powerful look at a life well lived!

Scott Catamas, founder, Love Coach Academy and Saturday Night Alive

Rajyo Allen, tumbled and humbled by life's circuitous, ever-changing, heart-expanding expedition, shows us in this raw, uncontrived, candid memoir that our wounds, imperfections and scars are also how the light gets out. Rajyo's entire earth walk has been a passionate, alchemical circumambulation around grace and love, both of which were held ceaselessly, fiercely and tenderly by unbreakable wholeness.

Rashani Réa, author, *Beyond Brokenness, The Fire of Darkness* and *Go Slowly, Breathe and Smile*

Fumbling towards Freedom is an intriguing and fascinating account of one woman's journey of awakening. The author shares many insights, which will be of great value to those seeking to find meaning in their lives. Rajyo showed remark-able courage, not giving up on her quest to awaken despite all the trial and tribulations of the journey. I highly recommend this book.

Leonard Jacobson, author, *Journey into Now* and *Words from Silence*

Rajyo Allen's brave and honest storytelling carves a path through the shadowy and mercurial elements of awakening. Her journey liberates the child within us yearning for freedom.
Jennifer Berit Wilson, co-author, *Order of The Sacred Earth: An Intergenerational Vision of Love and Freedom*

Rajyo expresses herself authentically and honestly with both her challenges and the insights she has gained. She is a true seeker who is willing to go to the depths and embrace the heights in her quest for freedom. And as a teacher, she shares her own journey humbly and fully so that others may also embrace the trials and tribulations of life and know all of it is an opportunity for greater healing, understanding and awareness.
Eudora Pascal, co-author, *Putting the Heart back in Business*

We follow the author through each rite of passage on her personal quest, from her wild youth to a maturing vision of what it is she is truly searching for. This book takes us on a journey to embrace and integrate all the struggles to find wholeness, peace and fulfillment. Anyone who reads this engaging and inspiring memoir will be convinced that she has certainly lived her life as fully as anyone. I am sure this book will inspire others to search for their own deepest truth.

Sarah Aspinall, author, *Diamonds at the Lost and Found*

This book is a testament to the resilience of the human spirit. Anyone looking for a roadmap to find their way home, will find the tools and inspiration within these pages. Thanks Rajyo for showing us all that no matter what, there is always a way.
Jennifer Hough, author, *Unstuck*

Table of Contents

Introduction

My journey is one of soaring to heights of ecstatic experience and diving to devastating depths, exploring the caverns of my soul, and shedding much of what I knew to be myself along the way.

I share what I have learned from my own experience.

Ever since I can remember I have wanted to know why human beings suffer, what causes this ache in the soul and the longing to be free. I have come to recognize that as human beings, we are on an evolutionary journey. I call it the "Alchemy of Awakening."

Each one of us goes through rites of passage, times of initiation by Life itself, testing times when we are asked to shed aspects of our personality and identity, and strip naked to face the new- the unknown—so we can grow and awaken in Consciousness.

For me, it has been helpful to embrace the idea of initiation, as a way to recognize and acknowledge how we gather wisdom.

My rites of passage have included making love for the first time, exploring myself through drugs and altered states, traveling the world on my own, finding a teacher, acquiring skills, becoming a teacher myself... and then, of course, letting go of it all and encountering death. Each step is a doorway to a new dimension of life.

Similarly, I have found it helpful to understand the phases of a rite of passage, which I can summarize like this:

Unraveling, when we are asked to let go of our old identity.

Descent, when sinking into the darkness of the unknown.

Limbo, when the old has gone and the new has not yet come.

Emergence, when we sense the new and begin to explore it.

Integration, when we find ways to live out and express the new.

I will not try to fit my story too tightly into these concepts – my life has been way too messy and chaotic to be confined to such a neat formula.

Nevertheless, I invite you to bear these concepts in mind as a reminder that every experience in life also offers a lesson to be learned, and an opportunity to mature as a human being. One more thing—when rites of passage happen in a timely, conscious, and contained way, they are usually positive experiences we can navigate and grow from. Birth, adolescence, relationship, childbirth, midlife, and death are all such initiations.

When things happen too soon and too fast, however, and are too overwhelming for us to integrate, they cause trauma which leads to coping strategies, such as self-abandonment and addiction. So please remember, in this tale, as I blunder my way from one transition to the next, that many times I was forced to change before I had the wisdom and maturity to embrace it.

And yet, through all of this, whether we know it or not, Grace is guiding us on a journey towards individual awakening and collective evolution.

And with our whole planet now suffering from our acts of ignorance, greed and exploitation—which threaten our very future—I think you will agree that a more mature approach to life is way overdue.

Here, in this book, I share the story of my grace-filled journey, my personal challenges and my own rites of passage. My wish is that my story gives you hope and inspiration for your own growth and awakening.

The Unbroken

There is a brokenness
out of which comes the unbroken,
a shatteredness
out of which blooms the unshatterable.
There is a sorrow
beyond all grief which leads to joy
and a fragility
out of whose depths emerges strength.
There is a hollow space
too vast for words
through which we pass with each loss,
out of whose darkness
we are sanctioned into being.
There is a cry deeper than all sound
whose serrated edges cut the heart
as we break open to the place inside
which is unbreakable and whole,
while learning to sing.

Rashani Réa

Chapter One
A Rough Start

The piercing screams of my little brother, Graham, erupted from the bathroom sending shock waves through my body. Just a minute before he had been sitting at the table with me eating his dinner,

"Mommy!"

"Mommy!"

Why was he crying so loudly? I wondered. I jumped up and followed my father out of the kitchen and into the bathroom. It was strange to see my beloved mother lying there under the water, blank eyes staring out at us, so cold and lifeless. I had seen her many times like this before at the end of her epileptic fits, but never quite like this. Underwater.

I saw the huge mound of her belly rising out of the water like a whale, still and silent, the child inside her, my unborn brother, bound helplessly to her, unable to free himself and find the life that was almost his. I couldn't understand why she was so still and how she could breathe under there.

My father gasped and stumbled, then quickly took us out of the bathroom, not saying a word about what was going on. My five-year-old mind decided Mama was in another one of her strange fits.

The neighbors were called, and we were shuttled off to stay with them. I didn't question what was happening; I was used to being the strong one and keeping it together when the world was falling apart around me. We were taken from there to my Auntie Betty and Uncle John's house in the countryside. It was all so strange, and no one would explain what was going on.

17

Why were we being sent away? Where were my mommy and daddy? Suddenly I felt more alone than I had ever felt in my life. I never saw my mother again and it was to be weeks before my father would reappear in my life. I was blissfully unaware of the gravity of the situation. We stayed with Auntie Betty and Uncle John for Christmas and into the New Year.

The Truth is Revealed

Little did I know that they were about to become my new family for a while. My father would drive down from London to the countryside on weekends. He would come into the house on a Friday evening, looking tired. I sensed the grief and overwhelm in him, even though I couldn't understand what had so suddenly changed. We had always been closely bonded and I so wanted to take away his pain, not even knowing what it was. One day we went into the large living room where my mother and father had celebrated their wedding reception. The celebration, just a few short years ago, must have seemed like a dream to my father now.

Sitting by the open fireplace, he took Graham and me on his lap and turned towards us.

"Mommy has gone to be with the angels," he explained.

"When is she coming back?" I asked in all my innocence.

"I... I don't know," my father said. He turned away to hide the tears filling his eyes.

He must have been beside himself with grief, and guilt as well, over the fact that he hadn't found her in time. He was completely unable to communicate the truth to us. I guess he thought that by not telling us directly, we would be spared the pain. Or maybe he just didn't know how to tell his kids that they had lost their mother forever.

And so, we moved between Aunty Betty and Uncle John's house, and the large country house belonging to Auntie Joan and Uncle Chris and their kids.

One evening Graham and I were taking a bath together, playing around in the bathtub. My cousin Nick, a few years older than me, came in. I splashed around and happily declared, "We're going to see mommy soon!"

"You don't have a mommy. She's dead," Nick said with the bluntness of a child who has no idea how his words are going to land. I screwed up my face and blocked my ears, not wanting to hear.

The Finality Sinks In

If the world hadn't ended at the sight of my mother's lifeless body in the tub, it ended with those words, even though my five-year-old brain didn't fully understand what "dead" meant or what that would mean for me. I knew there was a finality to those words and that scared me. Auntie Joan came into the bathroom and yanked Nick away, and I heard her scolding him outside.

It began to sink in that death had taken my mommy away and I would never see her again. In that moment the happy innocent child in me also died. I knew my life would never be the same and in a way my childhood was over. A deep sadness settled in my soul like a heavy cloud of unexpressed grief, and I knew from that moment on I would be always searching for what I had lost.

When my mother died so suddenly both Auntie Betty and Auntie Joan stepped in as surrogate mothers for a while, willing to take us into their homes and families while my father dealt with things in London. The apartment we lived in had been claustrophobic and frightening to me during my mother's epileptic attacks, especially when Graham and I were alone with her.

I would try to rescue everyone and figure out what to do; I was glad to get away to the spaciousness and fertile green of the countryside. We were happy to be there, away from London's grey skies and buildings and crowded city streets.

Unlike our small two-bedroom apartment looking out over the skyline of London, Winterpick Corner in Sussex and Rough Acres in Kent were large English country houses with sprawling grounds.

Comfort Amidst the Loss

Mostly we stayed at Winterpick Corner, and my cousins welcomed us into the fold, the eldest, Christine, taking special care of us as she was already into her teenage years. There was always a fire in the living room at my aunt and uncle's house, and the Aga stove in the kitchen would pump out heat to keep the house warm.

The house had many bedrooms, enough so that my cousins, myself, and my brother could have our own rooms, which was a real treat. Every bedroom was decorated beautifully—in the style of old English country homes—in warm colors with floral prints and matching curtains and bedspreads.

I remember waking up to the smell of oats cooking all night on the big old farmhouse stove. Breakfasts were large and lingering, with eggs and bacon and toast with lots of butter and steaming hot cups of tea. Tucked into the corner of the bench at the large kitchen table, eating my porridge, I would imagine that this was my family, and this was my home, the kind of home and family I wished I had, where everyone was present and there was a sense of normalcy, safety, and security.

There was always lots of laughter and play and two parents were present to take care of us kids. I think that's when I started to live in an imaginary world, dissociating from my normal reality into a more beautiful world. A happier place. I didn't know it then, but losing my mother was a wound that I would carry with me my whole life, making me feel somehow different from other people. I always felt that maybe it was my fault that she had died.

Chapter Two
In the Beginning

My mother had been an attractive and adventurous young woman who wanted to explore the world and had travelled from South Africa to London in search of a bright future. She was beautiful inside and out. Her graceful slender body, generous smile, and sparkling brown eyes got her a modeling job in London. Her radiance, innocence, and charm captured the hearts of many.

When she began waitressing in the coffee shop where young people hung out in the '50s which my dad managed, she captured his heart, too. He always had an eye for beautiful women. He chose her to be his bride, even though he had never wanted to settle down before. She melted his heart with her beauty, gentleness, and grace.

I don't know if he was ready to have a family—he was not yet thirty when they married—but soon, I came along, the first of what my mother hoped was going to be a large brood of seven children, just like her own family. She missed her family, and felt alone and isolated in London

My father also came from a family of six kids; I guess that was the norm in those days. I don't think he was excited about the prospect of bringing numerous children into the world, knowing what a responsibility it is to raise children and support a family. If it were up to him, he would have taken more time to build his business and establish himself in the world. But isn't that often how it is? The woman decides and the man follows, unwittingly, down her path.

When I was born, I was the sunshine of my mother's life, and she poured her love and devotion into the task of caring for me.

I was given the Afrikaans nickname of "Trinsky," which means "Little Angel." My father adjusted more slowly. Although he loved and adored us, I sense he had some ambivalence about having kids. But he always said that on that winter's day in February when I was born, the sun shone, which was a rare thing in London in the winter. He always saw me as his little light.

Then came my brother, Graham. It was during a visit to the hospital after developing Grand Mal seizures that my mother discovered she was pregnant with him. Her fits were scary experiences. I remember her lying comatose on the floor, unconscious except for the writhing body, frothing mouth, and eyes rolling back that turned her into some strange foreign entity rather than the safe haven of my own loving mother. The fits went on after Graham was born; he would be screaming and crying, and I would be trying to comfort him, saying, "It's okay Boetie (Afrikaans for "Little Brother"), don't cry, Mama's going to be alright." I was not at all certain she *was* going to be alright; I was in a helpless state of shock and panic myself but somehow I had to keep it together, so the rest of the world didn't fall apart. Already my coping strategies were in place.

Holding Back the Tears

That was how it was for me as a child. Being the eldest and the one who didn't have the same suffering as the rest of my family, I had to be the strong one; I had to keep it together. I held back the tears, the fears, and the confusion in order to take care of my little brother, and not let my mom or dad know how much I needed help. I needed holding. I needed comforting. I toughed it out. I knew I could help everybody else out by being a super child. I became very sensitive to the emotional tone of everyone else, learning to sense what was going on that was not spoken and how I could address those hidden needs.

Dad would be out working yet worrying all the time that something terrible was going on at home. He was in a hopeless situation. If he left work to care for my mom then there would be no money coming in, and if he stayed at work then we might be alone with her during an epileptic seizure—and who knows what might happen then? Perhaps she would drop us on the stone steps outside, or fall on us and suffocate us? I remember when he came home and I would see the worry on his face. I would ask, "What's the matter Daddy?"

"I am so glad you're okay," he would say, and breathe a sigh of relief. I know he had been holding his breath at work, wondering what was happening at home.

Taking Control

I became overly responsible, feeling that I needed to take care of my parents and my younger brother, none of whom were dealing well with our situation. I needed to take control, although it was not my job as a little one. I shut down the feelings of the vulnerable child inside. I stopped needing anything. But it came out sideways. I became petulant and willful when I wanted something. I substituted the need for tender parental love with a demanding nature.

My survival strategy was to take control in order to try to secure the love I needed. It was all I knew how to do at the time. The little one's needs for safety, support, and nurturing were buried in order to take care emotionally, physically, and psychically of everyone around her.

The situation was tense. As it turned out, Graham had been born with Still's disease, a type of rheumatoid arthritis that affects children, and I often heard him crying out in pain at night when he had to turn over in bed. He was a happy and cheerful little guy during the day, and even though he was a buoyant good-natured child, his days were increasingly compromised; running, jumping, and playing like the other kids was often a painful experience, as his growing bones were stifled by the crippling arthritis.

As a family, our days were spent in the hospital trying to help him find some ease for his condition. Every week he would go to the hospital to lie in baths of hot wax to soften and ease the pain in his joints, and at night he would have to wear splints on his arms and legs to stop the arthritis from distorting his growing joints. He also had to swallow huge pills that used to get stuck in his little throat. He hardly ever complained about the pain he was in, and he always found a way to laugh and play.

When we weren't dealing with Graham's pain, our days were spent dealing with my mother's illness. It was like being caught in a strange seesaw reality. When my mother was well, my brother would get sick. As soon as my brother got better, my mother would get sick. It was as though they were both playing out some strange karmic nightmare. My father was overwhelmed with worry and fear. He started losing his ability to cope.

Chapter Three
Alone

When a friend of the family from South Africa was visiting us, she saw my mother emerging from a fit, carrying Graham upside down, not knowing what she was doing. At any moment she could have stumbled and fallen.

My father felt that our lives were in danger, so he decided it would be best to send us all off to Africa, where my mother's mother, my Ouma, and so many loving aunts and uncles and nannies in mom's family could take care of us. My father needed to focus on work and earning money. And he needed a break. I didn't want to leave him. He was the one I felt safe with.

"Daddy, daddy, I don't want to leave you. I want to stay with you," I cried as I clung to him. I could feel him tense up as I held onto him tight. The pain of saying goodbye was hard on him too, but he didn't know what else to do.

"I'll see you soon enough my angel," he said, as he hugged me goodbye.

But it was not soon. It was many months before I would see my daddy again. I remember crying at night because I missed him so much.

"Where's Daddy? Is he coming? When are we going home?" I would complain to my mother. My mother would try to reassure me, but a part of me was always waiting to see my daddy again. In South Africa my mother and brother and I lived on the family farm on the African plains.

My mother's family was close-knit, and we were surrounded by extended family, as well. The local Zulu people from the village worked on the farm and I became particularly bonded with my nanny. She gave me another nickname, Makukorba (pronounced Ma-Ku- Korba, meaning, "She who walks ahead.") Interesting how the native people see these traits and name them so early on. This has been true for me my whole life: I stride out ahead.

Soon enough, this became my new family, and as kids do, I adjusted and became happy. We were enormously adored and cared for, and I loved the feeling of the vast open spaces on the African plains, playing with the farm animals and being with my mother's large family and their community.

However, after eight months, the time came for us to travel back to London. We went by ship, so the journey took several weeks. I couldn't wait to see my daddy again, and I remember running around on the ship's deck and finding a tall dark stranger who somehow reminded me of my dad. I became very attached to him and followed him everywhere. He obviously enjoyed the company of this bright little three-year-old. And yet, maybe he thought it strange that I was calling him, "Daddy."

Finally, we landed at Portsmouth Harbor. My father was there to greet us, and upon seeing him, I was overjoyed. I threw my teddy bear up in the air and went running to him.

"Daddy, Daddy, where were you? I missed you so much!" I cried.

"I'm so happy to see you, my darling child" he cried as he picked me up, spun me round and hugged me tightly. After this, I would not let him out of my sight. I would scream every time he left the house, crying in great fits and yelps of uncontrollable anguish. Mama tried to comfort me, but I would not be soothed. I did not feel safe; I was always afraid something bad was about to happen to her and I would be left responsible to make sure she was okay. It was an enormous pressure on me.

Constant Uncertainty

After coming back from Africa, we moved from our basement flat in Bayswater to a house on the trendy King's Road and then finally settled in an apartment in Forest Hill in South London. It was in a brand-new fancy block of flats up on a hill, with a stunning view of the skyline of London. My father loved to show it off to his visitors.

Our new home was the crowning glory of a lovely estate, with townhouses and lovely gardens in the center where us kids could play safely. There were parks and wooded areas just across the road. Here on the outskirts of the city, we were fortunate to have so much greenery around us, which was to become my refuge growing up.

We had been living in the flat for six months or so when we discovered there was a third child on the way. My mom had developed epilepsy when she was pregnant with my brother, and she was convinced that getting pregnant again would make the seizures go away. The medication she was taking in those days were contraindicated for pregnant mothers, so she had to live with the fits to protect the child in her womb. She didn't want to take the medication anyway as it made her feel depressed.

So, we all lived in a constant state of anxiety and uncertainty, never knowing when the fits would happen, at which time our lives would be temporarily disrupted.

Being the eldest child, I took it upon myself to turn Mommy over when she lay on her back during one of her fits, and I knew who to call when we were left alone with her. There was a time when we were on a bus in the center of London and she had a fit, and I somehow had to get help and find safety for all of us. I realized later how much the stress of all that cost my developing nervous system, and how much I would have to heal later in life.

My mother was days away from giving birth when we found her that tragic night. My father had prepared dinner for my brother and me and we were at the table. My mother took some time for herself in the tub before Graham would go in and be with her to do his nightly exercises, soothing his stiff joints in the warm water.

I remember sitting alone at the table, seeing my father's tired face as he came back into the kitchen saying that Mama had had her time alone, and was now ready for "Boetie" to go and get into the bath with her. My little brother toddled off happily to have his special time with Mama and do his exercises. The two of them had a special bond between them, united by their illnesses.

I was left alone with my Papa, who I loved dearly but who had recently started to seem distant and unreachable. I sensed the struggle and pressure he was under and tried to make things better for him. I so badly wanted to take the pain away from everybody and couldn't understand why it had to be so hard.

I developed a very capable little personality to cope with all of this. I remained calm when everyone around me was suffering. My father was going out of his mind with worry. My mother was happy most of the time but then would become very strange during her fits. Graham's disease meant he was often in pain.

Childhood's End

The night of my mother's death left us all with a burning pain that was simply inextinguishable, as if a wound had been opened that we never seemed able to close.

And so, my brother and I ended up spending weeks, which turned into months, with our relatives in the country. It was late November, and there was snow. Everything felt so pristine and perfect. I loved playing outside in the pure whiteness and then coming into the warmth of a world where I didn't have to know what to do, and I didn't have to be strong; I could just be a child again. I remember the feeling of being safe and warm and held, and I wished all my family could be there, too.

I didn't realize at the time that I was to spend much of my childhood in this or another aunt's home, and I would never have my own family again in the same way I had had before.

My childhood from that point on was spent shuttling between the comfortable country living of my relatives and the lonely existence of our London life. There, we often came home from school alone, letting ourselves into our cold apartment, with its creaky wooden floors and walls that whispered the memories of the suffering of its inhabitants. There was a blood stain on the wall where my mother had hit her head as she fell, reminding us of the pain and sorrow we had all experienced, more so now that she was gone.

Home was not a happy place for me, and I missed my mother terribly, as I gradually grew used to the fact that I would be growing up without the tender comfort, reassurance, and healthy mirroring of my dear mother.

I tried desperately to fill the void that my mother had left, to somehow become the wife to my father and the mother to my younger brother that they both needed.

I remember cleaning the house to try to create some order, and ironing my father's shirts for work, doing the best my five-year-old self could do to make everything seem normal and take care of everyone's needs. I didn't realize then what an enormous burden I had taken on and that it was not my responsibility to take care of everyone, and that I in fact needed the same kind of care and nurturing that I was trying to provide for my family.

On the flip side of trying to be an angel to everyone, I would fly into fits of rage or uncontrollable sobbing when the overwhelm became too much for my young psyche. I tried so hard to keep it all together and keep everyone from falling apart.

Fumbling towards Freedom / Rajyo Allen

Chapter Four
Ladies' Man

My father had always been the free spirit of his family, carving his own path instead of becoming part of the family business. He hadn't wanted to take on his father's shoe manufacturing business and had left as soon as he could. He became an entrepreneur, and he was constantly reinventing himself in business. Always a spiritual seeker, he was curious about the deeper meaning of life and who he was beyond the conditioned roles and responsibilities the rest of the world felt he should assume. In the late 1950s and early 1960s that was a radical outlook, and it took courage.

Instead of any kind of formal religious upbringing, I was raised on tales of the radical Armenian mystic Gurdjieff, and Dad was in a group with John Bennett, one of Gurdjieff's British students. Our bookshelf held books such as Gurdjieff's *Beelzebub's Tales to his Grandson* and *In Search of the Miraculous—Fragments of an Unknown Teaching*, written by P.D. Ouspensky, Gurdjieff's chief student.

Another Gurdjieff book, *Life is Real Only Then, When I Am*, sowed the seeds of my own inner inquiry into what Life is, what real means, and who am I, *really*? I didn't know it then, but this was the very beginning of my own spiritual search. The bond that my father and I had in wanting to know who we were beyond society's conditioning was there from very early on and would become a thread throughout our lives together.

I don't think my father ever really had time to grieve. He just had to cope with suddenly being left alone with two young kids to provide for, while still running a business. He never remarried; he never wanted to be tied down by a woman, even though that would've been easier for him and for all of us. He valued his freedom more than anything and I am sure he also struggled with unresolved grief and guilt. Overwhelmed with the new responsibility of single parent, especially as he did the best he could. Even so, my father managed to live a very full life, even with us two kids dogging his every step. He had his work, his various entrepreneurial endeavors, his spiritual pursuits and his female friends. He was a very attractive and charismatic man, with soft brown hair and blue eyes, a youthful body, and a gift for telling stories and jokes. He loved to throw back his head and laugh loudly, which I loved because it reminded me that the light was still on in my family. He had always been a ladies' man, even before my mom, and I think his female friends provided an escape and distraction from the burdens he was carrying.

Friends and Lovers

After my mother died, dad would often have his lady friends over for dinner after we had been put to bed. I was happy to see him have some company but was cautious about these new women showing up in our world. Oddly enough, the women he preferred were often like wicked stepmothers to us, and Graham and I vetoed them as fast as we could. And he didn't truly care for those that we loved and wished could be our new mommy. His girlfriends, as well as our nannies and au pairs, traipsed through our lives. Some were casual dates, and some became good friends over time, but only a few of them wanted to live with us and be our mother. Sometimes when my father took a lover, things would be easier for us. Several of his lady friends were constant in our lives, and he would enjoy long dinners and glasses of wine with them once we were in bed. And then there were the passionate affairs. I know he was a very sexual being and loved to make love. As our bedroom was right next to his, I would hear lovemaking going on into the night, long after I should have been asleep.

Graham and I really bonded with Andie, an actress on the West End stage, and her dog. She loved us and gave us affection and attention equal to what she delivered to my father, which felt really nice. Then there was Sandie. We really wanted Sandie to be our mom, but she was kind of crazy, an unusual type for my father to choose. We bonded with her young daughter, Michelle, who became like a stepsister to us, and we tried to include her in our little world. Sandie took Michelle and I to be child models, and that was a very bonding experience for us

The three of us shared our bedroom. It was cramped. And I would get angry with her when she did anything that would interfere with my world. I felt so little control over anything that happened, I had to get a grip somehow, even in small ways.

One night, as we were preparing to go away on a holiday with Sandie, there was a big fight over my brother, little Bootie, who was going to come on holiday with us. Sandie didn't want the burden of caring for him, and my dad obviously needed a break. Pots and pans were thrown, and the police were called. The next morning, Sandie, Michelle, and I left for a holiday at Butlins camp, leaving Graham and my dad behind. When we came home, Sandie's belongings had been thrown out on the street and she and Michelle were not welcome anymore. We never saw her again. It was another painful reminder that for me, a "normal" family— even one in which both parents fought—was not meant to be. I did not belong in that world. My world was different. It was my dad, my brother, and myself, all living in islands of our own pain.

No Mother Figure

I remember overhearing a heated conversation between my father and my Auntie Betty once.

"These children need a solid secure childhood. It's not good for them that you bring so many women into their lives, and they don't have a mother figure to care for them. Why don't you get married and settle down?" she said in exasperation.

"I am doing what I need to do for myself, and I make sure the kids are as well as they can be. I am not going to marry again just to provide them with a mother. I need to live my life as well," my father retorted.

After that our visits to Winterpick Corner and Rough Acres became fewer and farther between as my father evaded my aunts and their condemning attitude towards his lifestyle.

For us, it was a lonely childhood. We would often be waiting outside of school for him to come pick us up, and he wouldn't come for hours. Or we would walk home alone to an empty house, where we would let ourselves in by putting our arms through the letter box and releasing the door latch. We would feed ourselves cereal or toast for dinner, sitting in front of the TV until it was time to put ourselves to bed. Alone. I would lie in bed for hours listening for the sound of my father coming in the door and I could finally breathe a sigh of relief that he was home at last.

For the most part, we had to get used to our father not being around that much. Raising two kids on his own, when he could have given us up, was a heroic act for any man left as a single parent especially at that time. But I know it was challenging for him, juggling single parenting with running a full-time business. He often worried about being able to keep afloat and not go bankrupt. I remember answering the door to strange men in black suits who would ask where he was; they wanted to collect money from him. I know he worried a lot, and there were so many demands on him at that time.

Chapter Five
Wild Child

The result of being left alone so much without a mother to guide and nurture me, coupled with my dad's uncertainty over how to raise a girl, meant that I became a wild child. I was part of a band of friends who would play together and get up to all kinds of mischief.

One day, when I was nine or ten, we hid on a corner of the property in the housing estate we all lived in. My eyes were bright, and my cheeks were flushed with excitement as I issued my latest dare to my friends:

"I dare you to strip off naked and run down to the shops!" I challenged.

"But it's a mile at least!" protested my friends.

"Come on, don't be a chicken!" I said and I flung my clothes off and took off down to the shops. The parents of the other kids were very upset that I had been encouraging such naughty behavior and they told my father, who scolded me, saying that I could not just run wild and free and get all the other kids in trouble. I had to reign in my wildness and be a good girl.

I smirked, and inwardly said to myself, "I want to be free, and I will live as I want to, not as others say I should."

With my best friend Ruth, I got to live out my rebel side. She and I would play truant from school as much as we could, hanging out with friends and being crazy.

I was developing the independence that got me through my childhood which would be a strong driving force in my life.

Where our father may have left us wanting, our wonderful godfather, Uncle Bob, filled that void mightily. He simply adored us. He'd been very much in love with my mother, and he transferred all his affection onto us; he was our fairy godfather. Every visit was a feast of love lavished upon us.

My father would often forget our birthdays and Christmas was always a scramble, but when my godfather would come, he'd bring gifts and chocolates and shower us with everything that made childhood a happy place for us. The times we spent with him at his home by the sea were blissful times where I could at last be a carefree child again.

Cinderella and Her Horses

When I was twelve, I fell in love with horses and spent all my time at the riding school close to our home. I loved being around the stables, with the earthy smell of manure and the new family I found there. I could also avoid my father's latest love interest, Cindy, a beautiful young Sri Lankan woman who hated Graham and I; she was jealous of my father's love for us. She was like the wicked stepmother in the fairy tales.

Every day, when I'd come home from the riding school, Cindy would order me to take off my clothes before I came in the house, as I stunk of manure. She would tell me to do the washing up or some other chore, as if I were Cinderella. I refused to take orders from her. I fought her every step of the way and tried as hard as I could to drive a rift between her and my father. I hated her affected posturing, and I used to mimic her behind her back which made her super mad.

My father really wanted to be with this woman, although she was only seven years older than me. Graham and I really didn't want her in the house, so we made life hell for her. Our house was not a happy place at that time.

With her dark olive skin, her almond eyes and perfect features, my father supported Cindy to begin her modelling career and helped her find her place in the world. Eventually, she was taken away by her strict Sri-Lankan parents who wanted to marry her off to a nice Sri-Lankan businessman.

She still came back to UK with him and re-started the affair with Dad after the marriage. I, however, was very happy that she was out of our house

Heading into puberty I spent a lot of time at the local riding school where I learned to ride and care for the horses. Working with the horses was my saving grace. Their big solid presence, their unconditional love, and their gentleness had a calming effect on me, and in the exertion of working long hours and riding the horses, I was able to tame some of my own restlessness and feel a sense of power and agency in myself.

It was a secure environment, and I found a sense of family and belonging there. I'd be there every day possible, from morning until night, missing school if I thought I could get away with it. I would lock myself in the stable with my horses and talk to them, grooming them till their coats shone, and pouring my love onto them as they loved me. I loved to get on their broad backs and ride them, feeling in command of these huge animals and empowered in my life, free to ride the London streets or trot and canter round the park with the wind caressing my face and the elements washing my spirit clean. It was so much easier to relate to horses than humans, who were often so confusing. I found a place with the horses and the people who cared for them.

I was the favorite of the owner of the riding school. He taught me, and all of us, everything there was to know about horses. He said that no animal was ever born mean, it was humans that made them so. He used to rescue horses that had been badly treated and nurture them back to health. Jim was an old London gypsy whose father had driven a horse and buggy around the streets of Brixton, and he had taught Jim everything there was to know about horses.

I was devoted to Jim. I listened with eager ears when he would share his horse-knowledge in the lecture on Tuesday evenings after the horses had been put to bed. With the earthy smell of a pot of flax seeds cooking on the stove to feed to the horses, we listened intently to all Jim had to share. Huddled up in the "office," the one stable reserved for the business of running the riding school, I lapped up everything he taught me. He knew all there was to know about horsemanship and equine care.

Losing My Virginity

Jim was also a rascal, as cockney Londoners often are. At the end of each long day, he used to take several of us home in his truck, and I would always be curious to see who he would drop off first... and last. The last one got to be intimate with him sexually, there in the cab of his truck, fondling each other's genitals... It felt naughty but nice. It was our little secret. I never felt like I was being taken advantage of, only that I had a special secret with him. Barely in my teens I felt proud that Jim and I got to be intimate. Maybe many of the other girls did, too. I don't know.

I was starting to feel sexual and become interested in boys and relationships. Jim told me that I needed to make a choice, it was either boys or horses, as the horses needed so much of my time and attention, and I couldn't be out late at night with boys and show up at the riding school at 6:00 a.m. the next day and be awake and present. Some of us tried but we were often just too tired to do all the work that needed to be done: mucking out, sweeping the yards, grooming, and exercising the horses. I chose boys. I often wondered if I made the right choice. Horses would love you unconditionally. Boys would break your heart.

Across the road from our riding school was a rugby field and I started dating a twenty-one-year-old rugby player. I fell in love with his strong rugged body and his fearlessness. I lost my virginity to him when I was barely a teenager. I don't know if it was love. We had fun together before he went off to Africa to work in Mali and I never saw him again.

Chapter Six
Lost

Late one night—naked and quite drunk—I tore off down the street at top speed feeling glorious and triumphant, wild, and free. I was tiny, blonde, and just entering my teens at the time. I was quite the pixie.

I was picked up by some strange guys in a van and by some miracle, I was not raped. Instead, they brought me home and stuck me in the bathtub. Very kind of them. That's where I woke up.

Some of my wild friends and I had walked down to the nearby pub one night and I had drunk Pernod and blackcurrant cordial until it was coming out of my ears. Sweet. Sickly. Licorice. Alcoholic. And I loved it. My restless spirit had found a new outlet. Alcohol.

Things were very loose in England in those days. Everybody was always in the pub, and nobody ever checked how old anyone was. I don't know how many drinks I had that night but after the pub closed at 11:00 p.m., I took off down the street, tearing my clothes off and running naked past the shops. I didn't care. I wanted to be free.

When I was fourteen, I got a job in a pub and started working behind the bar. At the end of the evening, I'd often go with the owner of the pub to the gambling clubs on Park Lane and Mayfair, and come home in the wee hours of the morning. Nobody knew how old I was, and drinking became my escape route.

My best friend Ruth was a big drinker and together we had a wild time. Alcohol proved to be a great way to get high and escape the pain of childhood and the drudgery of school and homework. I always felt school and the things we were being taught were a waste of time.

Party House

When I was around sixteen it was clear that as a family, we needed more space. My brother and I needed our own rooms. My father bought a house and let us live there, while he continued to live in the apartment nearby. Our house became a party house and my crazy friends and I had some wild times there, especially when my father was away travelling.

Everything went on in that house—acid, mushrooms, alcohol, hashish, amphetamines, you name it. One party took place when my father had gone to Asia on business for several weeks. I remember the house was a crazy house, one person had put his arm through the glass door and the door remained broken for weeks while everyone came and went as they pleased. A girlfriend of mine had overdosed and was rushed off to hospital. There were people sprawled over couches and furniture in various states of drug-induced consciousness. All this was happening while my brother was studying for his O levels.

Graham and I hurried to get the house shipshape again as we awaited Dad's return. We prepared a nice dinner for him. Dad came in, went to the bathroom, returned to the table and sat down. As he raised his soup spoon to his mouth, he calmly asked, "What is that footprint doing on the bathroom window?" I stifled a giggle and checked to see if Graham was going to give up the ghost. I knew exactly what caused the footprint: a mere twenty four hours earlier, while on acid, we'd tried to see how many people we could cram into the 4' x 6' bathroom.

Although I didn't really like hashish—the refined version of pot—I smoked a lot of it because that's what everyone was doing. The thick black resinous substance had such a strong smell and an even stronger effect when smoked in either a joint, pipe, or a bong. It would immediately take me into an altered state and sometimes, if I smoked too much, I'd end up comatose on the couch. I often didn't know what too much was as I so wanted to fit in with all my friends who had a much greater tolerance. But I started to like the feeling of being here, but not here. It felt good to just check out and not have to feel anything.

My first acid trip was very telling, in hindsight. I was sixteen when someone handed me a small tab with a black microdot on it; I took it and placed it on my tongue. On our way to a party, my friends and I had to walk through the forest where I had spent many days as a child. It was a very interesting little forest, with ancient ruins and an old railway line running through it to Crystal Palace, the home of the Victorian period's Great Exhibition. "The woods" had been my refuge as a child. On this day, as my friends and I ran through it and down the long sloping pathway to the exit on the other side, I ran faster and faster, feeling so free, like I could actually take off and fly. My legs became wings and propelled me forward and upward. I felt I was invincible and that I was superhuman.

At the gate to the woods, we had to stop and straighten ourselves up as best we could, enough to walk down the street and cross the road to where the party was. It was one of those wild 1970s parties, where everything was going on, loud reggae music and, of course, alcohol, hashish, and lots of acid. By the time we got there, I was coming on strong.

A Bad Trip

Everyone's faces began to look weird. I didn't know how to relate to people anymore. It was my first acid trip, and I didn't know what to expect, or what was normal. Everything started morphing in my senses. I remember some of my friends tripping out with some sugar that was spilled on the table, it was alive, with the granules crawling and squirming all over the place. It was overwhelming, and I had no idea how to orient or ground myself. I started picking up random things: a cup, a roll of scotch tape, a spoon.... I was fascinated with each item, but then I couldn't put these things down. It was like I didn't know how. But it was more than that: I couldn't let them go. It started to freak me out – that I actually couldn't let these things go.

When my friends caught onto this, they thought it was hilarious. They were always up for a laugh and instead of checking to see how I was doing, they took the scotch tape and started taping all these random items to me. Eventually I was walking around with a spoon, a saltshaker, a cup, a notepad, a fridge magnet, and more, all taped to me. It was hysterical for my friends. Except it wasn't funny for me. I wouldn't call it a bad trip, but it was super intense because I saw something about myself. I didn't make the connection then, but in hindsight, I can see I was in a lot of pain, and it was the first time I got to experience my "attachment wounding."

Without secure parenting, I didn't know how to let things come and let them go. The loss of my mother and my attachment to my father was starting to play out. In my desire to party and feel free, I received a glimpse of what would become a strong theme for me: through all the changes in my life, I was desperately trying to hold on as everything kept getting ripped away from me.

I took it personally. I didn't understand that life is a constant cycle of endings and beginnings, of dying to the past and opening to the new.

Trauma occurs when things happen too much, too fast, and too soon and I would have to grapple with this. For years, I simply re-enacted that trauma by crashing and burning through life. Clearly, I was in terrible pain. I tried in many ways to get out of it by leaving my body, through alcohol, drugs, and sex, but Life was here to show me that there were things I needed to face inside myself, and that first LSD trip was a harbinger of what was to come.

Chapter Seven
First Love

My first boyfriend, Tony, was a beautiful guy, a real sweetheart. A Pisces like me, he was super mellow, stoned all the time, gentle, loving, and accepting. Everything was cool to him, he embraced life on its own terms, allowing things to be as they were.

He had long wavy dark hair, a soft smile, and a gorgeous body, with slightly bowed legs, making it seem like he was rooted in the Earth. He walked with a swagger as he glided over the ground. He always had a stoned grin on his face and no matter what was going on, nothing was a problem to him. He radiated a kind of spacious compassion that melted my heart. He was someone I felt I could be totally myself with and who would assist me to explore both my inner and outer world. With him I was able to live all parts of myself, the shy, freaked out, scared little girl, and the wild, outrageous, adventurous spirit. He loved all of me, and I felt I could trust him on a very deep level.

Tony was a free spirit and a gentle old soul, unfazed by life's ups and downs. Just as he allowed me to be completely me, whatever that was, he also gave himself complete freedom to be all of who he was, mostly dictated by his heart, but also by his desires and attraction to other women. He was, after all, half-Italian. And for some reason it was okay with me, I didn't feel threatened by it, I guess because he reflected back to me the free spirit in me, and I, also, loved to explore in different ways with different people. Growing up without the traditional role model of two parents and having a father who loved women, I never felt it was wrong to love more than one person. How limiting to think that only one person can fulfill all our needs and desires! But with Tony, I felt met on so many levels, and

43

we loved each other in all our facets. I loved making love with him, our bodies melting and our souls merging, sweet and deep, intimate, and easy.

While I was finishing my last year in school, with Tony away on his first trip to India, I had an affair with my art teacher. I loved art and my teacher saw the artist in me; it could come alive around him. As I was by that time in the Sixth Form—my final year of school—we had much more freedom and permission to do as we pleased, as long as we also studied and passed our final exams. My teacher and I used to hang out in the pub across the road from the school, drinking beer, and then afterwards we'd go back to his place and make love. I admit there was definitely an element of pride that I got to sleep with the sexy art teacher that everyone else had a crush on.

Life in the Squat

Somehow, I managed to graduate with A Levels in Art, History, English Language, and English Literature. When I left school, I also left home, and moved into a squat in the same part of London where I had grown up, down by the railroad tracks. Noel Terrace was an abandoned block of flats, with four stories and two apartments on each story. It was a wild place, and all my friends were living there. Our doors were open to each other, music was always playing in every apartment, no one worked, and we were all stoned most of the time. In those days in England, we were able to live off social security checks, and we were happy to be able to do as we pleased. Hashish, mushrooms, and acid were freely available. This was my first experience of communal living. I could go see Jerry and Brian, the cool dudes down on the ground floor and hang out listening to reggae music for hours, smoking joints, dancing, and laughing. I would spend many days and nights with my friend Tony, the snake man, with his skinny body draped in black leather and lots of chains. With his big sad eyes, long painted nails, and long brown hair, he looked like Alice Cooper and I was turned on by his eccentric authenticity. His passion was snakes; all kinds of snakes, from boa constrictors to pit vipers. We would get stoned or high on mushrooms or acid and listen to Bob Dylan, Patti Smith, the Velvet Underground, the Doors, Janis Joplin, and Jimi Hendrix, tripping out to the music and the sensory experience of the snakes slithering over our bodies, moving into a cool reptilian world of no mind. His place smelled of cigarettes, hashish, and snakes, not a very pleasant combination, but I was in love with this dark-haired and wild young man and the nether worlds we would enter together. It would freak me out when Tony would feed the snakes live mice, especially the venomous ones. But he had good protection with the chains he wore round his hands over the thick leather gloves. I felt the nearness of death with the danger he put himself through. It brought a subtle thrill to be so close to something so deadly. I was glad they were safely in their tanks most of the time.

High on Heroin

I lived on the top floor with two junkies from Australia: Pete and Butch. Of course, I started using too. We were high on heroin a lot of the time, melting into a stoned haze together. The three of us were lovers, all sleeping on the same mattress on the floor of the small room, sharing each other freely, our bodies intertwined as the heroin flowed through and between us in a world of music and heroin, tangled sheets and melting bodies. As the real world faded, I would enter a space inside where there was no separation, just a sublime feeling of completeness. Lying between these two men, I felt the boundaries between us melt into a sublime love affair where nothing but the experience of being completely free and totally at ease took over. There was nothing I needed or wanted except to be here with my two gorgeous men, getting high. We would lay around all day, making sweet mellow love, me in the middle with these two beautiful men. Pete was tall and handsome, with black hair cut in a punk cut, and Butch was small and dark with long hair and a softness to his face and body. They were best

45

friends, and I loved them both equally. There was no jealousy or possessiveness between us.

These were blissful times for me, albeit drug induced. I did not shoot up much, although they did, and there was a turn-on in watching the needle going into the veins and the immediate release as the liquid poured into them and carried them off inside. I loved the feeling of being here, but not really here, in between worlds. I could feel the pull of the heroin inviting me into its addictive embrace. But something in me stopped me from getting hooked, and I was glad later that I did not develop Hep C like so many of my friends who shot up in those days. Somehow my guidance was already on board in those days. It was enough for me to snort the seductive drug, even though it took longer to reach me.

All the music and drugs took me deep into an alternative world that was more fascinating and seductive than the dreary London streets outside Noel Terrace, where we would hear the regular trains on the railroad tracks outside carrying people to and from work in the city. We lived in a rich and colorful alternative world, outside of society, and I was feeling no pain.

Eventually Pete and Butch left to return to their native Australia. I was heartbroken and I had to kick my heroin habit fast. I did not want to get lost in this world alone. There were some uncomfortable days and nights of cold sweats, shivering and intense cravings, but they didn't last long, and as my main suppliers weren't around, I had no choice but to go through the withdrawals. Heroin had been a journey into the kind of peace and inner freedom I was searching for. But it was not what I was truly seeking in life. I knew there was more available to me, and I wanted the real thing. I realized I would have to give up the drugs and the temporary high they gave me and journey through the numbness and dissociation—and into the pain I had unconsciously been trying to bury—in order to find the true Freedom I was looking for.

Chapter Eight
Living Free

When I was in my mid-teens, my friends and I would take off to the countryside in the summertime, living on the land, travelling in a caravan from one free festival to another, from Stonehenge in Wiltshire on the summer solstice, to the fields around the ancient town of Glastonbury, then to the wild lands of Wales, living in each place for a time, then moving on until the autumn equinox when the weather would start changing and we would head back to the city and real life.

We would live out on the land for three months at a stretch, in tents or teepees, sharing food, and helping each other freely. We happily communed together in small groups of six or seven friends merged in with up to several hundred people in total. This gave me some of the happiest days of my life. Playing beautiful acoustic music, sitting around the fire for days and nights, dancing to the bands playing loud rock music on the various stages that were set up around the venues...we were so free, far from the rules and regulations of society. Of course, we took a lot of mushrooms and acid and smoked a lot of hashish. We had our own ongoing Woodstock festival, and I was in heaven. It was a rich deep time of intimacy with each other and the land. I went months without looking in a mirror, and I only washed when we found a stream or river to bathe in, I felt happy, healthy and whole. Being so close to Nature, with my new extended family. I found it easy to trust in life to take care of me.

I felt at home, far from the city and away from the world. Listening to our own flow and the rhythm of Nature, it was a wild and free life. It was always hard to return to the confines of my life back in the city, and I was yearning to adventure on into the unknown.

Passion for Truth

After a year, my first love, Tony, returned from his trip to India. With him I shared not only stoned nights but also a passion for the Truth and the search for what is real and meaningful in life. Through him I was able to appreciate the rich inner life that is possible, not only with drugs but also through spirituality. He would take acid, not just to get high, but to get to know himself in different realms of consciousness. He opened the doors of perception for me. I was happy when he returned from India. Tony's brother, Paul, lived in the countryside, a short train ride out of London, and most weekends we'd go down to the communal house Paul shared with his friend, Steve. There was always amazing music playing, as there was almost everywhere in the 1960s-1970s. The Moody Blues, Jefferson Airplane, Pink Floyd, The Grateful Dead. The living room was laid out with rich Turkish rugs, old sofas, and comfy cushions, and we'd spend hours zoning out on acid or hashish, letting the music morph our minds and expand our senses.

After journeying deep inside, we would enjoy plentiful cups of strong black tea and toast, or hearty homemade soups, and then go for long walks in the countryside. At the bottom of the garden there was an old dead tree, its bare branches reaching into the sky; it was like a Zen reminder of death in the midst of the rich green of the English countryside. There was a big sign hanging on it that said, "The Way." It was like a Zen Koan, a way of posing a question that cannot be answered by the rational mind, but drops you into a deeper understanding of the nature of reality. As I understood it, "The Way" was inwards. And out of one's own mind. And then whichever way you took became *"The Way."* I always remember walking out the door to the back garden and into the fields beyond.

My Inner Depths

On my first visit to the house, I was given a tab of acid and I knew I was travelling into the unknown. It felt so new and scary to be with all these experienced journeyers. I wanted to be able to trust that I could travel my inner depths too, without stopping short out of fear, staying in the safe and comfortable world of the familiar.

I felt safe with Tony and his brother's friends. But was I safe in my own inner depths? The old sense of insecurity was always dogging me: am I enough as I am? Am I worthy of being loved and seen for who I am? Can I trust that I will be safe and held no matter what happens? My inner world was sometimes a scary place, and I often felt the pain of growing up without the guidance and reassurance of a loving mother.

As I took the acid, I looked around at all these familiar faces. Things started melting, getting weird. I experienced all kinds of feelings in my body as my vision started morphing and changing. I looked outside and I so wanted to go out and run and play in the fields. But my body wouldn't carry me. I had to surrender to the powerful pull of the LSD within me. The feeling of fear gripped me and made me want to cling to a familiar sense of normalcy, but it was too late, I could not hold on. Pretty soon the fear gave way to an overwhelming sense of love and inner knowing that I was held in an infinite embrace. I was so small, yet part of this incredibly rich tapestry of light and color and sound. It became easier to let go and trust it, even though I had no idea where it was taking me.

Tony, Paul, and Steve were all seeking; searching for something else through the acid, hash, and pot and they were also interested in the wisdom teachings that were coming through. Books written by people like Ram Das and Alan Watts were saying that there's more to this life than we've been given to understand: question everything, wake up, step out of the mindset created by society, open up your Consciousness.

I started to see there's more to life than this perceived reality of bricks and walls and materialistic thinking. This was the first glimpse of my spiritual life, and it set me on a journey away from the world I had been brought up in. I became increasingly dissatisfied with the life that was being offered to me. The education I had been given was so small compared to what my soul was yearning for. I always felt that the school system was

49

geared to producing efficient little worker bees, capable of keeping society functioning on its most basic level, but it did not tend to the deeper needs of the soul, or to the evolution of Consciousness itself. I loved learning, but I hated being told what I should learn based on what would get me a good job. I longed to break down the walls of the life I knew and spread my wings to explore. I wanted to go to the places and meet the people who had the knowledge and wisdom I was seeking.

Hard Work, Good Fun

It all led me to India. With Tony having recently travelled back overland from his year in the Far East, I could see he had changed, and he had grown. I knew I wanted what he had found, so we made a plan to get to India as soon as possible. In those days you could travel around England and Europe picking fruit to make money. All summer we picked hops in England, grapes in France, and strawberries in Denmark. They were wonderful days of hard work and good fun around the campfire, eating the local food and drinking lots of beer or wine.

While we were in Denmark, we heard that Steve, who had lived with Tony's brother Paul, had committed suicide. Our friend John walked into the house and found him hanging from a light fixture. He had just returned from India and couldn't handle the disconnect between what he had discovered for himself in India and the drudgery of the limited life that met him in England. It was a shock and a new perspective. I had my first look at the other side of personal expansion, and it was a sobering reminder that we need to integrate what we find on the inside with our daily life.

This was also my first experience of having someone die, yet still experiencing them as omnipresent. Steve's body was gone but I felt his presence all around me, even in Denmark, far from where he had died in the English countryside. I became aware that death is not a finality: the spirit is simply set free from the confines of the body. I wanted to know what was beyond the veil between life and death.

Chapter Nine
India, My India!

By the beginning of winter, Tony and I had enough money to go to India. I was eighteen. We left with £500 in our pockets and a small backpack each, with just one change of clothes.

We planned on staying for a year and we wanted to see as much of India as we could. I was excited to be out of England, and off on my travels. My dad was fine with me going to India. He knew I was on a quest to find myself and he supported me in that. I was happy that Tony was by my side. He had been there before, and he could show me around.

When we landed in New Delhi, I was surprised that I felt immediately at home. We were thronged by dark skinny sweaty men in ragged clothes, all looking the same, all clamoring for attention, all trying to get us to buy a taxi ride from them. It was hard to feel the desperation of their need. I felt empathically overwhelmed by the poverty surrounding me and how hard it must be to survive along with millions of others in the same predicament.

But I soon came to realize and accept that this was India, and this was normal for people here. Back in those days, I was one of the earlier hippies, and white women in some places were still a rarity, so they grabbed for my attention.

Tony and I fought our way through the airport and out into the Indian air. The smells still catch in my memory, the heat, the staleness of sweat and human waste, mixed with the sweet fragrance of incense and chai.

We had flown into Delhi, in the North of the country, where it was still winter and quite cool, whereas we wanted to experience the warmer climate in the South. So, we took a train to Bombay—or Mumbai as it's now called—and then a boat to Goa, where we would meet up with Tony's brother and his girlfriend.

We had a limited budget and wanted to make our money last as long as possible, so we travelled as inexpensively as we could, often in third class with the poorer Indians.

I remember trying to sleep on the deck of the boat to Goa. I was squeezed tightly in between other people and I felt hands groping me in the dark as we as we sailed along in the Indian Ocean. I pushed them away in disgust.

It was a relief to wake up in Goa as the boat moored up at the dock—to hear the cawing of the crows, to smell drying fish and coconut oil, to feel the balmy air on my skin. We immediately stepped into a slower, more relaxed pace of life.

Simple Life

Goa was very simple then, just locals coexisting with hippies living on the beach. We rented an old Portuguese house for the next three months, not far from where Tony's brother Paul and his girlfriend were staying. They had a small baby and were happy to be bringing this child up free from the confines of British rules and regulations.

We loved being in Goa despite the accepted bouts of diarrhea and tummy upsets which we all got from time to time from drinking strange water and eating spicy food that may not have been that clean.

The lifestyle was timeless. We drew water from the well to cook and wash and spent timeless hours washing the baby's diapers and hanging them on the line.

We ate fresh coconuts and lived on the simple vegetables and fish we cooked, or the *puri bhaji* we got at the chai shop. We sat on the vast verandas of our Goan house left over from the Portuguese, who had only left Goa in 1961, just sixteen years earlier, so their colonial influence and affluence were still very present.

We spent long days on the beach, from sunrise to spectacular sunsets over the Indian Ocean. It was a blissfully simple life. Some people lived in bamboo shacks on the beach, living lives that were sweet and simple.

I remember the fishing boats coming in, where we could buy fresh fish from the fishermen, and the busy Goan markets where we would buy our vegetables and spices.

The smell of coconut oil was everywhere—the women's hair was coated with it, and it permeated the aroma of the food cooked on open fires. Coconut was a staple of our daily life, from the mattresses we slept on to the drinking coconuts with which we quenched our thirst. Even the alcohol we drank was made from either coconuts or cashews. I can still remember the nimble barefooted Goan men climbing the tall coconut palms, finding seemingly impossible toeholds with their broad feet, to tap the coconuts to make the fermented Goan drink, feni. I remember the red hills with the bright green cashew flowers and fruit, the fragrance of which was so sweet. It all felt so romantic.

I loved the simplicity of life in Goa. All we wore from dawn to dusk was a piece of cloth, called a *lunghi*, tied around us, and on the beach itself we were always naked. I felt so happy and so free from the restraints and constrictions of my western upbringing.

During that year, Tony and I planned to travel all over the Indian subcontinent.

From Goa, we went to the southern tip of India, and Ceylon, now called Sri Lanka. We visited the Buddhist shrines and temples in that beautiful, peaceful land with the sweetest chai and the hottest curries.

As I sat eating fruit for breakfast in Sri Lanka I would giggle at Tony, sweating, as he forced himself to consume the flaming curries people there eat at breakfast.

The beauty of the land there was breathtaking, from the ocean to the jungles, the rolling hills of the tea plantations, and the massive golden statues of Gautam Buddha.

We made our way up the east coast of India, through Madras, now called Chennai, where Tony almost died of a fever, which we later realized was malaria. He was delirious and we had to get him to an Indian hospital for treatment to bring him back. I remember all the sick people sitting in the corridors, and the rats running around the floors of the hospital.

Once, Tony opened his eyes just in time to notice a large air bubble in the syringe the doctor was poised to deliver to him. It probably would have killed him if it had gone into his arm. Fortunately, he survived, and we could travel on, although the malaria continued to bother him for some time thereafter.

Chapter Ten
Rude Awakening

From the heat of southern India, we made our way up to the mountains of Darjeeling and then to Nepal. There I fell in love with the Nepalese people. They were happy and kind, humble and compassionate.

Kathmandu was a simple place in those days. We stayed just off Durbar Square, and hung out in one of the many temples, where the lepers and hippies would gather. I made friends with all. We ate yak cheese and creamy lemon curd from large clay bowls, and the delicious apple and lemon meringue pies enticed many a traveler who was weary of Indian curry.

We took a bus to Pokhara, and when I saw the beautiful valley surrounded by snowy mountain peaks, and the lovely lake where the King had his summer palace, I thought I was in Heaven. It was so idyllic and magical: green grass and tranquil waters, corn fields and peaceful people.

The children would come running up to us, gleefully trying to sell us magic mushrooms, which we would take to a chai shop and ask staff there to cook us a mushroom omelet or make mushroom tea for us.

A while later, as if they knew exactly how long it would take the psilocybin to kick in, those same kids would come and dance in front of us, laughing and making weird faces and trying to freak us out.

We stayed in a small farmstead where the family grew corn and had water buffalos for milk. The mother fed us dhal bhat, a simple meal of rice, watery dhal and potato *sabji*, the staple of every poor Nepalese family.

The simple houses had clay floors and walls, and shutters for doors, but we were happy to be sleeping on beds strung with rope and covered with a thin coconut mattress.

The highlight of my time in the East was trekking in the Himalayas, walking through the incredible Nepalese landscape, wandering for days through valleys and forests, by rivers and gorges, gradually climbing higher across glaciers and through sparse mountain villages, towards those towering peaks of the highest mountains in the world.

Waking in the dark each day to a cup of chai made over a woodfire in the corner of a stone house, we'd be out walking by dawn, feeling a sense of peace and harmony to be in this timeless flow of life.

We'd walk for hours, sometimes together, sometimes alone, often with fellow Nepalese travelers; for the only way to get anywhere in those days was to walk. If you would ask any Nepali person how long to the destination, they would tell you *"Ek ganta"* meaning one hour. It was never true, and I never knew whether to be grateful or mad about that!

Sometimes it would take a week, sometimes two weeks, to get to our destination. There was such camaraderie and generosity among the people trekking, with smiles and greetings of *"Namaste,"* meaning "I honor the light within you."

Many Nepalese people walk barefoot, and their feet are like elephants' feet. They are hardened and tough, squashed flat from carrying heavy loads up impossible mountain paths and hopping on rocks over rough terrain. On the border between Nepal and Tibet, where no one has passports, the border control used to distinguish the Tibetans by their cloth boots, and the Nepalese by their bare feet.

Dysentery Hell

We wandered through the lowlands for quite some time before we started climbing. And it was at this point that I ran into serious trouble. I had taken a liking to Nepalese rice beer—called *Chang*—and although I didn't realize it at the time, it was brewed under beds in pots, with water drawn straight from the river, where everyone goes to poop.

It wasn't long before I was pooping my insides out, in agony with amoebic dysentery. There was blood in my stool, and I was throwing up violently, and in just a few days I had lost so much weight I was having to hold up my shorts to stop them from falling down to my ankles. We were trekking with another friend, Roger, who had to carry me part of the way as I was so weak.

Finally, we arrived in a village where we got a room and Tony and Roger tried to take care of me. I was so sick I thought I was going to die. I had never known such agony.

I was so weak I could not walk and there was no treatment for me in the village. There was no choice but to go back to Kathmandu. Fortunately, the son of one of the villagers worked for the Red Cross and took me by jeep back to the capital, where strong antibiotics killed the amoebas and got me on the road back to health again.

That was the end of my first trekking trip in Nepal. But I would return many more times to wander these high mountains and lose myself in the beauty of the land and the people.

I was very emaciated by this point. I began to take opium, because it has a constipating effect on the body, and it is also deeply relaxing.

Somehow, I managed to continue traveling. From Nepal, we took a bus and then a train to Dharamshala, a hillside refuge town where many Tibetans lived.

Tony and I both loved the Tibetan people and felt empathy and compassion for the plight of the refugees.

I knew he had lived in the little ridgetop refuge before, but I still wasn't prepared for what he disclosed on the train en route.

Rude Awakening

I was sitting next to him on the crowded Indian train on the way up from Delhi, when he turned to me hesitantly and said, "I have to tell you something."

"Tell me!" I said, surprised. We had never had any secrets from each other. He had even told me about the sexual encounter he had had with a sultry Indian woman in the filthy toilet of a crowded Indian train, while I was stoned out on opium, during a long three-day trip from one end of India to another.

"I had a lover in Dharamshala when I was last here, and she's probably going to be there."

I had never been a jealous type, so I shrugged.

"Why are you telling me this?"

"Because... I think I have a child with her."

"Oh," I said, feeling like the wind had been taken out of my sails. I struggled to digest the implications of this news. Lovers were one thing. Children were a whole other ballgame. At least I was prepared. Or thought I was. But was I able to handle it, that was the question?

We reached Mcleod Ganj, above Dharamshala, at the time still a tiny, bustling village filled with Tibetans in long robes with colorful aprons, their long braids tied with turquoise and coral beads. They turned their prayer wheels while mumbling the mantra, *"Om Mani Padme Hum,"* in deep undertones as they shuffled through the streets and walked the kora, circumambulating the Dalai Lama's Palace at the end of the town overlooking the valley.

I was still sick and frightfully emaciated, and not in my right mind. We stayed in the smallest and dirtiest hotel because it was the cheapest one available. "The Tibetan Memory" was owned by an old Tibetan man who had come across the mountains and who had lost most of his sight from snow blindness. His weathered face showed his trials, but it was lined with compassion.

On many nights, the villagers would crowd into the hotel lobby to watch movies on an old screen projector, drink yak butter tea, and chat enthusiastically with each other in Tibetan.

We rented a little room in a corner by the entrance, with only a curtain separating us from the busy goings on in the foyer. As we were out of money after a year in India, it was all we could afford: four rupees a night. There was very little place to be private, and I felt uncomfortable being in the middle of everyone's comings and goings.

I felt even more uncomfortable finding myself in the middle of Tony's relationship with Ruth, the woman he'd warned me about, who washed clothes for a living at the communal faucet opposite where we were staying.

Every day Ruth would come and seduce Tony's attention with her sideways glances and smiles. I didn't know what to do.

This intrusion into my relationship was very disturbing, and Ruth did not seem to care that Tony was with me, nor did she care how I felt about the situation.

I was still very weak, numbed out from the opium, and felt resigned to my fate. I had the feeling that whatever was going to play out would happen anyway. Pretty soon, it became too much for me. But I had no clue what to do. The village was intimate, and everybody knew what was going on.

I told Tony that if he needed to stay, that was okay with me, but I didn't want to be part it. At the same time, I was terrified to be without him.

I felt small and alone. I was sick and very weak.

I could see the Tibetans watching the drama unfolding, gossiping quietly among themselves, and gazing at me with compassion. Something had to change... but what?

Chapter Eleven
Turning Point

I started wandering outside of the village and into the cool mist of the Himalayan foothills, away from the dirt and dogs and people and the confusion in my mind.

The bright pink and purple rhododendrons coloring the hillsides and the snowy mountain peaks beyond soothed my soul and helped me to calm down.

On one of my walks, I met a real mountain of a man, my first "sannyasin," or follower of the controversial Indian guru Bhagwan Shree Rajneesh, who had taken the ancient term for the wandering holy men of India and given it new meaning.

He called his sannyasins "Neo-Sannyasins." Instead of renouncing their worldly possessions, including house and family—as was traditionally expected of someone who commits to this way of life—Rajneesh sannyasins would remain "in" the world, enjoying everything it had to offer, while dropping any attachment or dependency through meditation.

This was symbolized with three commitments: to wear orange robes, to wear a "mala" around their necks that contained a locket with a photo of Bhagwan, and to change their name.

My new friend's name was Himalaya, and how fitting it was! He was a tall, beautiful man. He stood like a mountain, with long thick, flowing white hair and beard, and flowing orange robes. He had a mala around his neck. He was slow and solid, and his presence was very calming to me. He became my rock.

To me, Himalaya was a god-like creature. From the moment we met, he took me under his wing.

Every night, we'd meet at the chai shop and talk for hours. He would listen to my ramblings and occasionally offer a pearl of wisdom that calmed my agitated state.

Meanwhile, I could feel Tony slowly pulling away from me, in his own struggle to do the right thing. One night, Tony turned to me and said "I am so sorry to hurt you. I don't want to lose you, but I feel I need to try to be a father to Anu, my little daughter. And for that I need to try to be with Ruth."

I had been preparing for this moment, the inevitable feeling of betrayal and abandonment. Numb from the opium, I looked at him with sad but glazed eyes and said:

"I know you are trying to do the right thing. I am sad to lose you, but I know you have to stay, and I have to go. I don't know if or when we will see each other again."

I'd had enough of being in the middle of this drama, and I had to do something about it.

I sought out Himalaya. He sat across the table from me, carefully sewing his orange robe. This was something everyone did back then because we only carried one set of clothes, and no one had the money to buy more.

I poured my heart out to him. He listened intently, as he always did, with a sense of calm and peace. Looking into his pale blue eyes, his presence was often enough to settle me, but this night I was really agitated and scared.

I was at a loss. I loved Tony, but I felt the right thing to do was to leave him to be a father to his young daughter, now just a year old. Shivering, even though it was not cold, I said to Himalaya, "I don't know what I'm going to do."

Himalaya looked up from his sewing and gazed straight into my eyes. "Later you'll come to the ashram to see Bhagwan," he said, "But first you need to go back to the West and get your health together."

He smiled lovingly and continued his sewing. His calm detachment soothed me. He was right, and I knew it. I was in a terrible state, and if I stayed in India, I might not live to tell the tale.

Healing at Home

Himalaya gave me some money to get a bus back to Delhi.

Along the way I met other sannyasins who also invited me to go and see this mysterious guru called Bhagwan. I had no idea what they were talking about, or what the big thrill was, but I found it interesting that I kept meeting these lovely orange people with wide open hearts and twinkles in their eyes.

As for me, my heart was breaking, my mind was hanging by a thread and my emaciated body desperately needed healing. Fortunately, I still had a return plane ticket back to the West, otherwise I was penniless.

When I arrived back in London, I was horribly thin and gaunt. Like some of the water buffaloes one sees in India, the skin was hanging off my bones. My father, bless his heart, was ready for me when I came home. It was as if he had known I was coming.

Before I reached the top step of his apartment, exhausted from just carrying my backpack, the door opened. My father smiled a warm welcoming smile and hugged me tight, and I could feel that I was home.

"I just put the kettle on." he said. "Come on in."

I was home once more. As constricting and claustrophobic as his small apartment was, it was what I needed at that moment: a womb to hold me, a place to come back to myself, and put the fragmented pieces of my body and psyche back together.

But he and my brother got a shock when they saw the skin hanging off me, covering the bones and veins of my skeletal frame.

63

My emaciated body was a physical demonstration of my broken heart. I questioned if I should have stayed and fought for my man. I wondered if I could have done something different. I didn't realize it then, but this would become a theme in my life: where and when to fight for what I loved and believed in, how and when to let go and surrender to the hands of fate.

I needed time to sort it all out, after this epic and life-changing journey in India. I was thrown into a deep hole inside myself, faced with a desperate sense of aloneness.

My man was with another woman, and I was here alone, with no drugs to fill the void or numb the pain.

The old sense of unworthiness I had felt while growing up, that I had tried to numb out with drugs and alcohol, came back to haunt me.

Too Small for Me

The freedom I had felt now turned into a horrible sense of constriction and limitation in London.

I tried to connect with my old friends from before—Tony the snake man, Ruth, and the old gang from Noel Terrace. Familiar and loving as they were, everything felt old and tired, and too small for me.

I sat in the pub which used to bring me such a sense of simple comfort, to be with these dear friends, chugging down a nice pint of draft beer. But now it felt flat and boring. My friend Tony, the snake man, looked at me from over the rim of his beer glass and said to me:

"In the olden times, people never went out of their village, they lived and died with the same few faces around them. They knew who their community was, and they never imagined anything beyond it. It was enough."

My stomach turned over with a feeling of horror. This would never be enough for me. His deep soft brown eyes, that I loved so much, touched me and I wished in that moment that this life and these friends could indeed be enough.

I burst into tears. I felt so stuck. I could not go back to my life as it was before India, and I had no idea how to move forward. I didn't know if my old friends understood, and I could not explain.

I had already lived way outside my village; I had been to the other side of the world and seen much that had changed me. I couldn't go back to being satisfied with a life in the pub down the road. The restlessness in my soul was clawing at me.

It took me six months before I could feel relaxed and comfortable in my body.

Lots of good food and rest helped me integrate the experience and gradually I was able to face the world again.

My friend John recommended that I take some yoga classes. I went with him to my first class in Blackheath, in southeast London.

The teacher guided us into various physical shapes, and I was amazed at how these postures, along with breath awareness, brought my mind into a deeper stillness and presence. All the fragmentation in my mind and disharmony in my body transformed into a sense of peace and vibrant aliveness.

I started doing hours of yoga daily as part of my healing and recovery.

I had found a key to an ancient memory in me, one of wholeness and balance and inner alignment with a deeper source.

What magic was this? I needed to explore more, not just through yoga but through my whole connection to India and the Mystic East. I had to go back.

Chapter Twelve
The Ashram

I arrived at Bhagwan's ashram in India just before my twenty-first birthday, on February 24, 1980.

I had taken a plane to Mumbai and was overjoyed to smell the familiar atmosphere of incense and stale urine, and to see the bustling crowds greet me. Once again, I felt at home here. Now I knew how to navigate my way through the throng of taxi drivers clamoring for my business, find one to take me to Dardar—the nearest station—and take a train to Pune (formerly Poona), where the ashram was located.

For the next six hours, sitting on a hard wooden third-class seat, I reflected on what had brought me to this point, and the unknown journey on which I was about to embark.

After several months of healing in my father's home in London, I had gone to Amsterdam, hoping to earn enough money to go back to India. I continued to do many hours of yoga and meditation in the mornings, and in the afternoons and evenings worked in the East West Center, a macrobiotic restaurant where I received further healing for my body with traditional Japanese food and remedies.

Somehow, I felt guided by a hidden source, even when I had no clear sense of where I was going, or how I would get there.

I knew, however, that I had to go back to India. I told my friend John who had been my yoga friend in London.

"I'm going back to India, and I don't know where to go. I'd like to come with you to visit your Tantric master." I knew he had a spiritual teacher who lived in a small village outside of Bangalore.

Fumbling towards Freedom / Rajyo Allen

"I'll check with Guruji," he said.

And he did. But the reply came back:

"Tell her to go to Bhagwan."

I was surprised and a little anxious to go to this strange ashram in Pune on my own, but also remembered the free and happy sannyasins I had met at the end of my last trip to India. I told my father I was returning to India. He looked at me with concern.

"Are you sure you are doing the right thing? You came back from India so emaciated. I'm worried you may get sick and die".

"Don't worry dad, I'm stronger now. I have my health back and I don't intend to do drugs. I'm on a spiritual quest. I know this is the right thing," I reassured him.

Strangely, it was my father who reaffirmed that Pune was the right place to go. He had been going through a hard time in his life, tired of the drudgery of work, and was on his own inner search for meaning. A friend of his had recently returned from Bhagwan's ashram and now went by the name "Aniketa." He wore flowing orange robes, long hair and a beard, and a mala round his neck. My father found these dramatic changes quite intimidating but began to read the books Aniketa brought back.

Little did either of us know that twelve years later my father would join me in the ashram and also take sannyas.

Of course, I started reading those books, too. *My Way, the Way of the White Clouds* was a book that really spoke to me. It lit the fire of longing in my heart to find the kind of inner freedom that Bhagwan was speaking about.

My Bamboo Hut

Arriving in Pune, I asked some sannyasins where I could stay and was directed to a small bamboo hut in the middle of a field, in the back streets behind the ashram.

My hut was one of three located behind the ashram. My flimsy door was held by a small lock and inside there was nothing but an Indian rope bed with a rough mattress. I paid 100 rupees a month for it. This was to be my home now.

I walked the short distance to the ashram along quiet residential streets of Koregaon Park, the suburb of Pune where Bhagwan and his disciples lived.

Pune had been a hill station that allowed officers of the British Raj to escape from the heat and dirt of Bombay. This part of the city was indeed very peaceful, and I was eager to explore the ashram itself.

The ashram had been purchased in 1974 by Bhagwan's followers. It was a grand old colonial mansion, and since then more adjacent buildings had been purchased to house Bhagwan and his closest followers, as well as the ashram's many facilities.

Other buildings held offices, shops, the post office, and the residences of some of Bhagwan's closer disciples. Other large houses on adjoining streets provided a place for the group work and the kids' school.

Directly ahead of the front gate, down a path that led past the main office, was Lao Tzu House where Bhagwan himself lived. It was always guarded by handsome hunky guys who kept people from flooding into Bhagwan's living space.

Lao Tzu house also held Chuang Tzu Auditorium where Bhagwan would hold intimate meetings of up to thirty people each evening. He would offer energy darshan—or blessings— or arrival or departure darshan, or group darshan for those completing certain groups.

But for larger gatherings he would meet us in Buddha Hall, a large open-sided auditorium with marble floors and a canvas roof. We would gather there daily to sit in blissful meditation with him and listen to his discourses.

Garden of Eden

The moment I walked through the massive wooden "Gateless Gate," the grand entrance to the ashram, I felt the different energy of this place. The Gate was flanked by the handsome guards—who I later learned were called "Samurais"— standing with their long flowing hair and orange robes.

It opened to a marble walkway surrounded by lush gardens and the whole place was vibrating with a kind of scintillating energy I had never before experienced. It was like a Garden of Eden, with many tropical plants providing rich color and a divine coolness to the atmosphere.

People sat in a relaxed manner and watched others coming and going, or chatted with a friend while sitting on a low wall nicknamed "the Zen Wall." Or I'd see them quietly meditating in the gardens.

Friends meeting each other would often hug for five or ten minutes, and I could feel the timelessness of the moment as their bodies touched, their breath synchronized, and they melted together.

In this place where there was nothing to do and nowhere to go, there was an air of freedom and permission to simply be oneself, I was struck by the image of so many happy smiling people walking through the ashram.

Mind Blowing Meditation

The moment I paid my ten rupees to get into the ashram, which was the daily fee, a whole new world opened for me, and I knew I would never go back.

I was so excited to explore everything. For example, I had heard about Dynamic Meditation, the wild cathartic meditation that happened at 6:00 a.m. every morning.

Of course, once again I had come to India with very little, so I didn't have a clock or know what time it was, and cell phones were unheard of in those days, so I couldn't sleep for fear of missing the meditation. I awoke every hour, wondering what time it was.

In the end, I got up in the dark and walked to the road where a lone *chaiwallah* sat on his haunches, brewing sweet milky chai for night owls. I sat with him drinking the hot chai until the first signs of dawn and then rushed to the ashram gates, with many other saffron-garbed people who were running, cycling, and arriving in rickshaws to the ashram.

Dynamic Meditation blew my mind. I was enormously impressed by the master technician of Consciousness, Bhagwan, for creating it. His meditation moved me through five stages:

Deep, full, fast chaotic breathing through the nose.

Full-on emotional catharsis: expressing the tears, the sadness, the repressed anger and rage, the gibberish, the madness, whatever arose to be expressed.

Jumping up and down shouting, "Hoo! Hoo! Hoo!"

On the word "Stop!" freezing on the spot in absolute stillness.

Dancing and celebrating as the sun's first rays came pouring through the trees, and the first bird calls were heard in the garden.

I was blissed out and fell instantly in love with the place and the people. With Dynamic, my mind had been emptied of its rubbish, my thoughts had quieted so my heart could speak, and my body felt vibrantly alive. Wow, what an experience. And this was just the beginning!

I went to get a chai and sat on the wall as sannyasins in their beautiful long flowing robes started coming into the ashram, to head to their various workplaces, or to meditate, or just to hang.

There was a lot of hanging out that happened on the Zen Wall and I was just beginning to learn the noble art of doing nothing.

Fumbling towards Freedom / Rajyo Allen

Chapter Thirteen
My Heart's Home

Bhagwan's whole intention was to decondition us from the seriousness and structures that had imprisoned us in the world. He wanted to create totally alive and free human beings and encouraged us to be as spontaneous and natural as we wished.

There were no rules and no "shoulds" or "have to's" here. Bhagwan encouraged his people to be a melting pot of connection, intimacy, and love. Long hugs of ten-to-fifteen minutes were common all over the ashram. We would often feel attraction and chemistry with the person we were hugging and find ourselves making love soon after. Love was free, and it was abundant.

Sitting on the Zen Wall drinking my chai, I noticed Himalaya gliding up to me with his long white hair cascading down his shoulders. He smiled as though he knew I was coming. I was so relieved to see him as I didn't know anybody there yet.

"Hey, I just arrived!" I said, "It's my twenty-first birthday and I have no one to celebrate with."

Himalaya chuckled. "Good! Let's celebrate together. I'm five!" he declared, meaning he had been a sannyasin for five years.

That evening, we celebrated together by going to Prems, the Indian restaurant where most sannyasins ate. A short walk from the ashram, it was located on a wide spacious street and shaded by ancient trees. Like many places in that area, it was basically a patch of earth fenced in with bamboo, although the kitchen itself was housed in a building.

We ate *palak paneer*, rice, and curd in the candlelit garden. This was all so new to me and yet, somehow, I felt completely at home here. The conversation was easy and relaxed, and I felt the warmth of Himalaya's heart.

Afterwards it felt natural to spend the night together in my little bamboo hut out in the field. We quickly became lovers. No commitment, no expectation, just an easy natural meeting and melting of the heart and body, for as long as it felt good and right to both of us. We just went with the flow of our own energy and how it moved between us.

In Paradise

In those days, many people lived in makeshift bamboo huts. Others were fortunate enough to rent rooms inside some of the Koregaon Park mansions, those old colonial homes that had once housed British officers and which had been left to slowly run down by the impoverished Indian princes who had moved in when the British Raj departed.

While I was there, sannyasins occupied several of these houses, living in all the rooms, on the balconies, and in the servants' quarters—even building tree houses in the garden—and decorating them simply, Zen-style, with colored cloth and photos of Bhagwan, bringing a sense of sacredness that reflected the inner beauty we all felt around the Master.

Walking to and from the ashram was easy on the wide tranquil streets. The pace was slow and unhurried, with sannyasins walking hand in hand, or cycling leisurely along, or, if a faster pace was needed, flagging down a passing rickshaw. It was a pleasure to walk under the acacia, magnolia, bougainvillea, and neem trees, enjoying the beautiful flowers in the gardens, with the sound of the exotic birdsong serenading me, their distinct songs piercing the silence. There was a particularly shrill bird that always seemed to be declaring: "Far Out! Far Out!" which was my experience exactly.

I was happy to be in the ashram. I knew I had found my heart's home and I never wanted to leave. At the same time, for some reason I didn't feel ready to take sannyas and renounce my worldly identity. With hindsight, I can see it was my own stubborn ego, holding on to my past, afraid to let go into the new and the unknown.

Green Girl in an Orange Sea

Before coming to India, I had become a Sufi. Back in the UK, at one of the free festivals, I had hooked up with a bunch of Sufis and resonated with their longing to merge with God, whom they revered as the Beloved within the heart. Just as sannyasins wore only orange, these Sufis wore only green, the color of the heart chakra, and it was also my favorite color.

When I arrived in Pune, I continued to wear only green. In a sea of orange people, I really stood out, which I guess is something I've always enjoyed doing. I'd walk into the ashram, one green girl in a sea of orange. While some people loved it, others wondered what I was doing there, but their curious looks and comments didn't bother me. I was having a good time, and was enjoying the meditations, the connections with beautiful men, and some lovely girlfriends I met.

Connections were easy and flowing. Friends and lovers were abundant and everything was centered around our love for the Master, our desire to live in his commune, and a shared vision of a different way of living and being.

We embraced the full spectrum of life in the ashram, every moment was an exciting new adventure. "Life is a Mystery to be lived" Bhagwan used to say, "not a problem to be solved."

With the mind quiet and the heart open, tears flowed easily, whether they were releasing old hurts and wounds, or simply tears of joy and laughter, the cornucopia of our beings were overflowing and life was an incredible dance.

Fumbling towards Freedom / Rajyo Allen

Chapter Fourteen
Being with the Master

Sitting with Bhagwan was an amazing experience. There was always a sense of magic in the air.

We all knew why we were there: to drink in his fragrance and steep ourselves in the perennial wisdom of the mystic. We were freed from all man-made schedules designed to keep society running according to the rules of the vested interests, the priests, and the politicians—whom Bhagwan labelled as outdated and ludicrous hypocrites.

By contrast, Bhagwan embodied and exemplified the freedom of living on one's own terms, according to a higher principle. He could talk for hours on any subject, about any spiritual tradition, from Jesus, to Buddha, to Lao Tzu, to Zarathustra. He could expound on the lives of these great sages and glean the insights that were relevant for us. At the same time, he would also tear down the elaborate façades created in their names, saying that the rigidity of the religions which followed in their wake were strategies to control and manipulate people. He often contradicted himself, so there was nowhere to stand and no way to hang your hat on anything he said.

Most of all, he kept telling us it came down to our own experience. YOU are the Buddha, YOU are the Jesus, "You have it all within you," he told us repeatedly. By the way, this was something he did not contradict! He did say we were buddhas—fast asleep and snoring, but buddhas, nevertheless.

Sitting with Bhagwan in meditation, all sense of separation disappeared and only a pure state of Being remained...open, empty, and free. Whole and complete. Nothing missing. It was a marvelous experience to live in the energy field of his ashram—the "Buddhafield" as we called it—journeying deep into our own inner consciousness, and at the same time having so many friends and lovers to play and explore with, learning to live and love more fully, and to be free.

Being with so many crazy seekers—lovers of truth, rebels without a cause, rejects, misfits, and outrageous outcasts—was unique and wonderful. I was constantly in awe of how we had all been drawn like moths to the flame of this mystic Master. There was much love, laughter, and intimacy, and many hugs, and heart connections, all shimmering in the collective silence of hundreds of silent souls meditating together.

Ecstasy Beyond Sex

In evening darshan, Bhagwan would meet with twenty-to-thirty of us in special energy sessions. While musicians played wild music, he would touch us on the forehead, give us *shaktipat*—a powerful form of spiritual transmission—and we would enter vast and unfathomable realms of Consciousness.

At such times, his female mediums would be dancing in wild abandon around him, channeling his energy through their bodies. It was an experience of ecstasy that looked very much like orgasm and yet it was beyond the sexual realm. For the rest of us, we would be dancing to live music in Buddha Hall, played by sannyasin musicians, and I was always at the front, dancing my way into ecstasy.

With the daily program of meditation techniques running almost continuously from morning 'til night, another state of consciousness permeated the field. Meditations were going on in Buddha Hall all day, every day. I would be hanging out with friends then pop off to do a meditation, connect with the silence within, then come back and have a meal with somebody, then pop off and do another meditation. If I wanted, I could meditate all day long. Bhagwan was a master technician of Consciousness. He knew that the modern mind is so tense, stressed, and full of neurosis that it cannot be still or silent.

That's why he created active meditations where we could express and release through dance, gibberish, or some other crazy thing to empty out our mind, body, and emotions, and then land in the most profound stillness of meditation. No map, just a direct experience of the territory. This stillness pervaded the ashram. There was a rich and juicy energy field surrounding everyone and everything we did. And when stuff came up, as it inevitably did, around relationships and sex and changing partners and more existential questions, Bhagwan would be available to answer, guiding us into deeper levels of awareness.

Or he would send us off to do a group and work it out therapeutically. The groups were radical and were held mostly in underground cellars beneath the ashram, where it was cool, and the walls were padded so that people could release the repressed energy without hurting themselves or others.

In those days there was freedom to really tune into what the moment presented and what we felt like doing. Bhagwan invited us to follow our own bliss... all the way to freedom. We were a fairly intimate crowd in those days. There were maybe up to a thousand people in and around the ashram, all involved in different ways. People were working in the ashram: cooking in the kitchen, cleaning rooms, gardening, creating malas, doing construction, running the post office and the shops, but it never seemed like work. It was always play. People would either work, or do groups, or spend time meditating or just hanging out. Each evening, it would all stop, and we would come freshly showered and changed to sit intimately with Bhagwan in darshan, or dance wildly in music group in Buddha Hall. The energy was very high as the whole field moved into ecstatic union.

Naked and Utterly Known

Ordinarily, Bhagwan only came to Buddha Hall in the mornings, to give his daily discourses. But on special celebration days he would come in the evening, and we would sing and dance in his presence. On one occasion, I was standing at the back of Buddha Hall, dancing wildly to the music and as it reached a crescendo, I felt Bhagwan's eyes on me. I opened mine and our eyes met. I felt him see right into me and through me. I have never felt so naked, or so loved. I knew that every part of me was known and accepted just as I was. At that moment, I also knew who I was. There was nothing missing and nothing wrong. In that moment I could have died and felt totally fulfilled. I was in ecstasy. It was at that moment I felt the urge to take the leap and take sannyas, to die to who I knew myself to be. This is what I had been seeking for my whole life, to be loved and accepted for who I was, no part left out. I felt Bhagwan knew me personally and had been calling me home.

Born Free

The kids, of course, did not have any structures or schedules apart from being at the school, so they were free to run wild. At the time, this seemed like a good thing. It was only later I learned that some of these kids suffered their own kind of trauma because, even though they had many adults loving and caring for them, ongoing contact with their own parents was at times missing. Late at night, I would often find a kid sleeping in the arms of one of the Samurai guards at the gate, and take them home to sleep with me, bringing them back into the ashram the next day.

The solid sense of security and protective boundaries, which all children need in their formative years, at least until they feel ready to move out into the world on their own, was not always present. The commune was supposed to provide this support, shifting focus away from a child's total dependence on the parents, but it didn't always work out that way. The kids did have a lovely school, where they were allowed to let their creativity arise, and the teachers guided them towards the subjects they found most interesting. In my experience, these kids grew up to be special human beings, with an intelligence and maturity beyond what you see in children who came through the traditional education system.

80

Chapter Fifteen
One Big "Yes!"

While the kids may have been trained to freedom, we older people had a lot of conditioning to unload.

Almost every group in which we participated was about taking the lid off repressed energy, bottled up inside us since those times when, as children, we had been taught that we must be nice, or good, or quiet, or obedient, that we mustn't say what we think, or do what we want. At the ashram, all of that was tossed out the window, and we were encouraged to be totally authentic.

When people came to Bhagwan, the first thing they were told was to participate in a couple of groups, in order to unload some of their internal baggage. The best therapies, and the most cutting-edge techniques, were imported from the West and the ashram soon became known as the Esalen of the East, named after the Esalen Institute in California, which at that time was noted for being at the forefront of the human potential movement. In the ashram, we had Breath groups, Tantra groups, Primal groups, Art groups, Meditation groups, and many more.

In the groups, the group leader would invite everyone to take off their clothes. In this, I felt right at home, as I loved to be naked. There was no room for shame or hiding. It was confronting for many people, as there was no longer anywhere to hide, but it was also healing as we were all there together in our nakedness and vulnerability. I remember the first group I did was in one of the old colonial mansions. Entering, we took our clothes off and left them outside. The weather was hot and sticky, so I was quite happy about this. Even the group leader was naked. We sat in a circle on mattresses that were covered with clean sheets. The group leader was a tall and handsome guy. He simply sat there and waited to see what would happen. In a very calm way, without saying or doing too much, he let the energy start bubbling up.

Within a short amount of time, people were sharing, crying, and raging, and by the end of the morning session they were either fighting or making love. There were no limits.

At the end of the day, the group leader gave us our homework: find someone you don't know and spend the night with them. I looked around and did not see anyone to whom I was attracted, so I made a beeline for the group leader and said, "You. I'd like to be with you tonight." He smiled and said "Okay, sure." We spent an amazing night in his balcony room with the gentle Indian breeze blowing through the mosquito nets and his strong arms holding me after we had made sweet love together.

Full Permission–No Inhibitions

On other occasions, given similar tasks, I wasn't so enthusiastic about the person I ended up with for the night, but it always gave me interesting insights into my preconceived ideas, my attachments, and my resistance. It was always freeing, radical and amazing. It was a grand adventure and I felt liberated by it.

There was no part of me that thought, "Oh, this shouldn't be happening," or, "they shouldn't be doing this." It was all just one big "Yes!" for me. Everything around Bhagwan was an opportunity for us to see our personality reflected to us. I loved the fact that people had so much permission to take the lid off. Normally, there is so much inhibition, so much possessiveness, so many rules, so much that we're not allowed to do. In the ashram we were free.

Of course, this would bring up a lot of psychological issues to be worked on, like anger, jealousy, and fear, and Bhagwan would chuckle at the process. He would tell people which groups they needed to do, and always encouraged meditation, reminding us that our freedom lay in our aloneness, not in our problems and issues with other people.

Everything at the ashram happened within a meditative energy field, so everyone would need to remember to come back to themselves, again and again. And be guided by the Master to a place of self-remembrance and consciousness. But first, all of that repressed stuff had to come out.

At one point, I participated in a Satori group. It was held on an ashram rooftop and lasted ten days. We sat across from a partner, asking and answering the question, "Tell me who you are." At first, I babbled all the usual responses about where I came from and what I did, but my list of items that made up my superficial identity soon ran dry and then I saw myself coming up with creative answers "I am a tree," "I am the ocean," "I am the sky," etc.

After many days, the thinking process was exhausted and the answers surprised me, coming from somewhere beyond the mind. "Peace," "stillness," and "silence," were some of the words that came. I felt freed from the mind and able to move into a state of inner freedom where I could taste my true nature, free and unbound.

Fireworks and Broken Hearts

Still, along the way, in this intense process, there were a lot of fireworks, broken hearts and even, dare I say it, a few broken bones from fighting in the groups. For example, if you were a jealous person and attached to a certain relationship, or you thought that your lover was yours to have and to hold, it was very confronting when they didn't come home at night, or you saw her, or him, walking down the ashram path holding hands with somebody else. Bhagwan would tell us, "You don't own anybody. Who is this that says, 'They're mine?'" His perspective was always beyond the dualistic.

We gradually let go and opened up, and then let go and opened some more. We got to taste real love, beyond society's norms of relationship.

Real love is not attachment and it's not conditional. Real love is not, "I'll love you, if you do this, or that, or are a certain way that suits me" When you tap into real love, your lover can come and go, and if they come again, you can be grateful, but if they don't, you can still love them.

I have so many lovers and friends from those days—really good friends—and we continue to be in each other's lives and hearts. It makes me sad to see what happens to relationships in our normal culture, with such ugliness and bitterness around separation and divorce. Everything becomes strategic and vengeful.

I was never a jealous person. I wasn't brought up that way, and I didn't have parents who were glued to each other, telling me I'd grow up, fall in love, and get married. I didn't have that modeling from my father, so it wasn't a strong part of my conditioning. Jealousy was never really my thing. I had many lovers in those days, freely coming together and freely moving on. Beautiful times with lovely men, and precious moments of fleeting love shared blissfully.

Through Bhagwan and the ashram, I found family, belonging, and the great blessing of a spiritual master. His words landed in my heart and in the deepest part of my being. I felt the truth of his statements; nobody else was speaking like this. It brought me so deeply into connection with myself and I understood what's possible for us all, the potential that we have in this life.

It included the sex, the play, the intimacy, the friendship, the work, the meditation, the adventure, the laughter, the tears... everything. That's what was unique about Bhagwan. He was a Tantric master. Tantra in the sense of embracing and including everything, so that no part is left out. That was radical. The dark and the light, good and bad, meditation and creation, life and death.

I remember his famous quote: "I am one with all things. It is easy to love Jesus, Lao Tzu, and Buddha. But what about Genghis Khan, Stalin, and Hitler? Only the anguish of such a realization can revolutionize life on Earth." This was the first time I had heard anyone speaking about embracing everything, bringing all parts of our humanity to our total divinity: totally in the world, and yet not part of it.

Bhagwan Versus Iyengar

To think that I could have ended up at the nearby ashram of BKS Iyengar, author of the best-selling yoga manual "Light on Yoga.'" He was also in Pune, on the other side of town.

I loved yoga and wanted to deepen my yoga practice, but Bhagwan and Iyengar were about as opposite as you can get. Iyengar was also a master, but he was a strict disciplinarian, and a rule-oriented conservative. So opposite to Bhagwan! Iyengar followed the Hindu tradition. He felt there was a right way to do things and a wrong way to do things, including which way your big toe was pointing in a particular yoga posture! If I'd gone there, it would have been a very different experience. I'm sure I would have rebelled or left pretty quickly.

Fortunately, I found my way to Bhagwan's ashram where the freedom my soul was yearning for was met and encouraged. I continued to do yoga, but all the rules were out the window at that point, there was no "should" at all. That was what I loved about Bhagwan. He was so vast. He included everything. Buddha, Jesus, Lao Tzu, all the teachers and the teachings, and in terms of personal growth every possible modality, tool, and technique, and we could choose which one felt right for us.

There were so many ways to explore. You could choose to dive into work in one of the many ashram departments, or you could do groups, of which, like I said, there was every possible kind, and all for a much cheaper price than in the West.

I did all the meditations, several groups, and then dove into working in the ashram. I was put to work in the kitchen, which was called "Vrindavan," named after the place in India most associated with Krishna. It was a very alive place, and we laughed and joked as we washed and chopped and cooked veggies and served food all day to the commune.

Being young and beautiful, I got swept up by many men, and I had many lovers. Most of the experiences were beautiful, but I don't think I really knew who I was, or what I wanted. I was like a leaf in the wind. But that's true of being twenty-one anywhere, isn't it?

Chapter Sixteen
I Am Ready!

My real joy lay in listening to Bhagwan's discourses, when I would often enter a deep space of silence and inner peace. But at other times I felt fierce resistance, my mind fighting with the whole idea of being his disciple.

I didn't want to be identified with this bunch of strange orange people. My stubborn ego wanted to maintain my individuality and sovereignty, and I couldn't see that I was holding on to a false identity. Bhagwan was waiting to give me the real thing, the experience of who I really am, beyond name and form. I remember him saying that, in ancient times, in the traditional master-disciple relationships, the student had to work hard and wait many years to be initiated as a sannyasin. But Bhagwan was giving it to us immediately, because today's generations—particularly in the West—lacked that kind of patience, commitment and dedication.

Nevertheless, I held out for several months, enjoying life in the ashram, and seeing Bhagwan every day. Gradually the love affair deepened, and as my heart softened and opened, I began to think more seriously about taking sannyas. No one pushed me; it was a shift inside of me. One day I knew it was right. I was sitting on the balcony with my beloved friend Buddha Prem (meaning "Buddha of Love"). He was a beautiful and slender man with big dark eyes, long dark hair, and a beard. His torso was bare and tanned, and he had just a *lunghi* wrapped around his hips.

I suddenly said to him "I am ready! I'm going to ask for sannyas."

I walked to the ashram and just as I got to the gate, there was a flurry of activity as Bhagwan's Rolls Royce drove out. This was very strange. Bhagwan never left the ashram. The most he ever drove was between Lao Tzu House, where he lived, and Buddha Hall, where he would speak to us. It was a distance of about 150 meters. He hadn't been outside the ashram gates since his arrival in March 1974, about seven years earlier.

Where Did He Go?

"What happened? Where is Bhagwan going?" I asked.

I was told Bhagwan was leaving the ashram permanently. No one knew where he was going. But he was definitely gone! It was a shock to all of us, to be left in this ashram without his guiding force in our lives. And, as you can imagine, I felt more than a little foolish that my stubborn ego had held out just long enough to miss receiving sannyas from the Master himself.

Still, I had finally come to the place of surrender, a little too late to receive it from Bhagwan directly. But Teertha, one of his closest disciples, gave me sannyas one evening in a small ceremony on the lawn next to Lao Tzu House, where Bhagwan had lived. I was given the name Ma Anand Rajyo, which means "Kingdom of Bliss".

"What a strange name!" I thought. I could not relate to it. The inside of my mind felt more like a prison of misery, filled with judgments and suffering, and not at all blissful. But my friends reassured me that it was okay, I would come to love my new name in the end. So, finally, I had a new name, orange clothes, and a mala with Bhagwan's locket around my neck. It felt like I had found something real, that I belonged to this melting pot of people from all over the world, gathered around the wild vision of this crazy master.

I had had no direction for so long. I had spent years trying to lose myself, or find myself, through drugs, alcohol, sex, travel, food or fasting, and any other avenue I could find. The trauma of losing my mother at such a young age, the feeling that I was unworthy of love, the agony of attempting to bury the lost child within, the years of feeling adrift… all of it began to ease as I recognized I had found something real and abiding.

Is This Who I Am?

I had begun to heal. Here I was: "Kingdom of Bliss." Imagine! Me? I was stepping into a whole new world. I threw back my head and laughed into the night at the cosmic joke of it all.

My birth name had been Jeanette; it came through my mother's lineage. In South Africa, if you called out the name, "Jeanette!" you'd see a lot of women and girls come running, from my grandmother down to me, my cousins and their children. But I didn't feel connected to that lineage. I never felt the name suited me. Nor had I ever felt that London, where I grew up, was my real home.

Not my name, not my place. And yet, when I finally did take sannyas and received my name—Ma Anand Rajyo—things finally began to fit. It was a completely different identity. Bhagwan had seen into my soul and recognized my true nature. Beyond the new name, taking sannyas marked a new beginning. By this time in my life, I had been through many rites of passage, as we all do, as we grow from being a child, to a teenager, to an adult woman. But this time it was different. Very different. I was doing it knowingly. This was my first conscious rite of passage, and it gave me a whole new sense of myself. At last, I felt like I had a true family. Soul family. For the first time I felt like I truly belonged. Everyone was free to be themselves, and yet everyone belonged to a larger context. It was so different from my upbringing in London, where there had been little spiritual context and no room for the sacred in my life. Yes, I had received glimpses from my father, from books, through drugs, or tribal gatherings of hippies, but my soul always felt hungry for the real thing. Now my life had meaning because it had a spiritual context. This would become the guiding principle for the rest of my life: to follow my heart, to trust the inner call for freedom, and to keep going deeper inside myself. Bhagwan had given me the greatest gift: for the first time my life had meaning and purpose.

And just at that moment, Bhagwan left! As I saw him driving out, naturally, I couldn't help but wonder what was going on. Soon enough, we learned he had gone to the United States.

Big Changes

His devoted secretary, Ma Yoga Laxmi, such a tiny woman in her body but so big in her devotion and energy, had been replaced. Her own secretary, Ma Anand Sheela, a young Gujarati woman who'd lived and worked in the United States, had been permitted by Bhagwan to step into Laxmi's shoes. The gossip was that Sheela was looking for land for a big new commune in America. This made sense, because, as hundreds more people were arriving and wishing to stay around Bhagwan, the ashram in Pune was bursting at the seams. Koregaon Park was flooded with orange-robed sannyasins. Since Bhagwan was so controversial, and since the process of buying land in India seemed so complicated, establishing a new commune here seemed almost impossible. Sheela's strategy was to do it in the USA where no one could stop her. She asked Bhagwan to go along with her plan and, in June 1981, he agreed.

Despite Bhagwan's move to the US, I was obliged to stay in India, mainly because I didn't know where to go and I had no money. The ashram had become my life, and this was where I wanted to be. But, on his instructions, Bhagwan's people had started dismantling the ashram, taking down all the temporary structures that had been erected around the old mansions and selling off tons of equipment. It was clear this phase of Bhagwan's work was over, but what would the next one be?

Chapter Seventeen
Retreat to the Mountains

I left Pune and headed for Goa, where I met many friends and could live easily and cheaply. From the beach, I tracked Bhagwan's progress as best I could and learned he had taken up temporary residence in a castle-like mansion in New Jersey, just outside New York City.

Within a couple of months, Sheela had bought a huge ranch in Eastern Oregon. Bhagwan had landed there and one year after his arrival in America he was calling for a big festival to be held at this new place, known as the Big Muddy Ranch. He called this gathering "The First Annual World Celebration," and it was to be held in the early days of July 1982.

Everybody was trying to get to America for this festival and, naturally, I wanted to go and be with all my friends—my family—so badly. But I had no idea how I was going to get there. I had no money to do so.

By March the heat in Goa was becoming intense and I retreated to the Himalayan foothills in Dharamsala, to my beloved mountains. It was there that I met Anu, the daughter of my first real boyfriend, Tony, with whom I had traveled to India. It had been just a few years earlier, but it seemed like another life – so much had happened to me in between.

I wondered about Anu when I arrived back in the little hilltop refuge of the Tibetan people. I didn't see her mother, Ruth, at the washing station, anymore. I soon learned she had fallen into bad ways, hanging with hippies, smoking chillums filled with hashish, and drinking. I guessed she was prostituting herself.

But I never saw her with her daughter, so I grew concerned and went looking for Anu. Ruth lived down a small alley in a tiny windowless room. I pushed the door open and there sat Anu, in a pile of filth, alone and neglected. She had a few pieces of bread but no real food. I know Tony had been sending money, but it didn't seem as if it had been getting through to Anu.

Unexpected Godmother

Impulsively, I made the decision to take this little girl up to my home in the hills. I lived with other hippies in a beautiful colonial compound overlooking the valley and the river below. It was an idyllic scene. I had a small room with just a bed in it and an extra room where I did my yoga and cooked simple meals.

Suddenly, I had another being to care for. She didn't know me but for some reason she trusted me and the kindness I offered her. It felt good to be able to look after her; it was the only thing I could do.

For several months I fed and cared for her, while an angry Ruth ranted and raged at me, sometimes even spitting at me in town. But she never tried to get her daughter back. I had no idea how to care for Anu in the long term. What would I do with this half-Nepali toddler? I knew I could not take her back to the West with me, so I made the decision to give her to a Tibetan family.

Tibetans love children and they had been watching what had become of Anu's mother. I was not ready to be a parent, or go through the whole adoption process. Besides, I had very mixed feelings about becoming a mother. Since my own mother had died, I did not trust my mothering instincts, and I was afraid that I would inflict a similar abandonment wound on this child.

In the end, I handed her over to a Tibetan family who ran a restaurant in town. They lovingly took her in and integrated her with the Tibetan community, where she grew up happily with the other Tibetan kids in the Tibetan children's village. She grew up thinking she was Tibetan, not knowing anything about her past. Years later, I went back to see her, and she had no idea who I was. She was happy, well-loved, and cared for, and I was free to continue my journey, knowing I had done the right thing for this little girl. She would have a good life.

Living in Limbo

 Meanwhile, there I was, in monsoon time, with the rains pouring down, the mountains misty with low hanging clouds, and my mood beginning to sink as I had no idea how I was going to get to America, where my sannyasin friends were heading.

With no other option, I made the best of my life in the mountains. I did a lot of yoga and meditation and continued to live a simple life, watching, waiting, and wondering what was going to happen. This was a time of limbo for me, and the only thing I could do was surrender to the mystery and trust.

One day, when the monsoon rains were particularly strong, I gave shelter to a young American woman who had been walking in the mountains. As I made her a cup of hot milky tea and we sat eating Indian cookies, we started talking about yoga, and which styles we practiced. In her, I felt I had a sister, someone who also had the same passion for yoga that I did.

I told her I was longing to get to America and attend the festival in Oregon. In reply, she told me she was from Los Angeles and added, "I'd like to help you." She said she would sponsor me to get a visa and loan me some money for a ticket, which I found totally amazing. My heart filled with joy as I realized I had the means to join the celebration in Oregon.

The Himalayas have always been an auspicious place for me. Each time I needed to leave India, the help came when I was in the mountains. Somehow, there was a sense that divine grace was showering on me and guiding my life, although, of course, more challenges were in store.

Chapter Eighteen
Landing on the Moon

"Where the hell am I? Where have I landed?" I thought to myself as I looked at my strange new surroundings. Everyone here seemed to be well off materially but disconnected emotionally and spiritually.

"Their hearts are closed, and they are in so much pain!" my empathic senses told me.

But it wasn't just the people around me who were in difficulty. It was me, too, arriving in America feeling small, lost, and alone.

I had lived for such a long time as a hippie in India that I didn't even have shoes on my feet. Really, it was a wonder they let me in the country.

Sarah, my American friend from the mountains, had loaned me the money for a flight ticket and sponsored my visa application, and everything had flowed easily, so I sensed that things would continue to work out for me in the United States.

That's how it was around Bhagwan in those days. The master's magic filled our hearts with trust and there was a grace that pervaded every aspect of our lives.

When I had flown into Seattle, I had been regarded with suspicion by customs and immigration and my baggage had been pulled apart, but I was eventually given the all-clear— there was really nothing to find, as I had brought virtually nothing with me.

After I had been allowed into the United States, which was a miracle in itself, I had flown to Los Angeles, and arrived in Beverly Hills.

Sarah did not have a place to offer me, as she had only just arrived back from India herself, but she found a room for me with a family that she vaguely knew. I felt like I'd landed on the moon, and I am sure those people thought they'd taken in a Martian. They were a dysfunctional version of the all-American family. The father was absent, the mother was "out of it" on prescription drugs, and the kids were watching TV pretty much all the time. Nobody communicated unless they were yelling at each other.

Everyone felt disconnected from everyone else, whereas in India everyone had seemed somehow connected, even if they were poor—there had been so much human interaction, so much friendliness and kindness. I had gone from the blissful experience of being with friends and lovers, whom I regarded as my close-knit family, to an American family that didn't seem like a family at all. It was like I had landed on an unknown planet and was trying to converse with aliens.

Wandering the Streets

I wandered around Hollywood and Sunset Boulevard. This was strange because nobody walks on the streets in LA. Everybody drives and there are only fast-moving cars and freeways that take you from one location to another. It was strange for me, for sure, after the bustling life on the crowded streets of India where I had felt completely at home and where everyone is friendly. Here everyone felt so separate, living in boxes, travelling in boxes and no one really relating to each other. I had no idea how I was going to get out of there. It was a long way from Beverly Hills to the Big Muddy Ranch in Oregon and I had no money, no friends, and no idea how to move forward. It was one of those moments in my life, when I had to trust the unknown and wait for guidance.

It was a challenge because I really couldn't see my way ahead, and I began to worry that I wouldn't make it to the Ranch in time for the first festival, due to take place in a few weeks.

One day, I was walking along Sunset Boulevard when I was approached by a strange guy. He looked creepy, but he persisted in talking to me. At twenty-two years of age, I was still quite gullible and innocent. He said to me, "You look like Olivia Newton-John. Do you know you could make a lot of money as a lookalike?"

Seeing this as my chance to get to the Ranch, I jumped at the opportunity to make some money and get out of this LA nightmare. He took me back to his place and said, "Take off your clothes. I need to see your body."

I started to get suspicious.

"I don't see why that is necessary, if it is my face you're interested in," I answered.

Then he grabbed me, threw me on the bed, and raped me. I didn't know what to do. I was out of my depth. Nobody had done this to me before. I felt it was better to surrender than to fight him, as I was afraid he could get violent. His smooth-talking, friendly air had evaporated, and his face now looked sleazy and disgusting. I smelled his aftershave as he pressed his face up against mine and forced himself inside me.

I was stunned that I had been so naive as to believe this guy. Yet he had sounded so convincing. Of course, I'd been well aware of rape when growing up in the UK, but it had been only through reports in newspapers and TV. After experiencing it myself, I was horrified that such things can happen to women and girls, ruining their innocence, destroying their trust, and turning them into victims of trauma. I had been sexually promiscuous in my life, but there is a definite line between permissiveness and force. The whole experience was confusing, because, like I say, I'd never been exposed to such sleazy tactics and deception before.

Venice Beach Connection

Naturally, after that horrible experience, I became less trusting and less gullible. This was my first taste of how things could be in America, which, I was beginning to realize, was a more aggressive and arrogant culture than the East. In India, I could walk anywhere on the streets and feel completely safe.

Even with teeming masses of sexually repressed men ogling me, I never felt like I could get hurt. But after this experience I realized that America, even in the middle of the day, can quickly become unsafe.

Everyone was seemingly nice, with big smiles and calls of, "How're you doing?" But no one stopped long enough to hear the answer.

People shouted greetings of, "Have a nice day!" but no one actually cared. Everyone had their own personal agenda in this glitzy world of LA with its dog-eat-dog mentality. In India, even the beggars had somehow been part of the whole web of life, and they were the ones, when I literally had nothing, who shared their food with me. Mother India takes everyone into her great burgeoning bosom. After I was raped in LA, I became more cautious, especially when walking on the streets alone.

Fortunately, I soon found my way to Venice Beach where I met an English guy, Dave—a big burly dark-haired man who smiled easily and had a great sense of humor. I knew I could trust him when I heard his accent. He introduced me to a friend who owned a nightclub who offered me a job as an exotic dancer.

All I needed was a bathing suit and some good dance moves—I certainly had a repertoire of those, having danced every day in the Pune ashram—and I had no problem getting naked and showing my model-thin body. In this context, I felt safe to do so. I found it fun and exhilarating to express my sensuality on stage, writhing about, turning on the male spectators as I took off my clothes, taunting them with my naked body. In three weeks, I had made enough money to get to the Oregon Ranch.

Chapter Nineteen
A Whole New Chapter

I took a plane to Portland and in the airport was guided to a fleet of old yellow school buses, driven by sannyasins, who were ferrying hundreds of arrivals from all over the world to the festival at Big Muddy Ranch.

As soon as we left the big city, I breathed a sigh of relief. My body relaxed and I began to get excited about this next chapter and what was about to unfold. After a couple of hours heading up the Columbia River, then into the Oregon back country, the bus rolled up to the crest of a range of hills, and the driver stopped to show us the land that was to be our new home.

"Pretty much everything you see from here is part of our Ranch," he told us, adding that the property extended over a hundred square miles.

I looked out towards the horizon and all I could see were thousands of acres of natural rolling hills and valleys, with no buildings in sight. We were on the "dry side" of the Cascade Mountains, and it was mostly semi-desert rangeland, with brown grassy slopes dotted with juniper bushes. It was hard to imagine then, that in a few short years we would turn this place into a luxurious oasis.

We trundled down a long, narrow, dusty dirt road into a valley where most of the Ranch buildings were located. We parked outside the Welcome Center and sannyasins came out to greet us with enthusiastic hugs and smiles. I marveled at the extremes I was experiencing: from my isolation and loneliness in Los Angeles to the relief of being back with my family at the Big Muddy.

A few things were different: sannyasins whom I had seen in Pune dressed in long, flowing orange robes, were now working in the Welcome Center wearing smart, dark red Western suits, pants, and skirts. Red had somehow replaced orange as the official sannyasin color. It took me a moment to adjust to the new look. But I quickly fell into the arms of my dear friends and sobbed, feeling grateful to be back in the grace of the Master's energy field. I was overjoyed to see everyone's happy faces.

Gathering of Hearts

Those that were already living on the Ranch had been working hard to get everything ready for us, and sprawling tent-cities had been erected to accommodate us. My first morning there I woke up and looked at the sleeping sannyasins beside me, feeling like a kid, who can't wait to get up and see what this day would bring.

I looked out at others, crawling out of their tents to stand and stretch as they headed to the rows of porta- potties, and then off to breakfast and a day of meeting old friends from all over the world.

In India, we had been free and easy hippies, with the laid-back lifestyle of the East, with no demands or expectations from society. Even though the situation was very different here we were thrilled to be together again with Bhagwan, with so much land to build a new commune with no limits.

There was great optimism and enthusiasm in the air. This was another exciting adventure with the Master. I had no idea what was about to unfold: that we would be working our asses off to create a city for 3,000 people in a desert in less than four years and then, having succeeded in our goal, we would watch the whole thing fall apart.

The first festival was a gathering of the tribes, friends arriving from all over the world to be together, eating, hanging out, sharing stories about our recent travels and adventures. And of course, sitting with Bhagwan in meditation in the huge Rajneesh Mandir that had been erected in time for us all to gather. He was in silence, so he did not speak, but there was stillness, music, and dancing, and so much joy and celebration.

I particularly enjoyed our "drive-by" events—so different from the LA application of the term to the shooting of people from cars—when thousands of us would line the roads winding through the Ranch, a long bright red ribbon of people, and greet Bhagwan with music and singing as he drove slowly by in one of his Rolls Royces.

The climax came on Master's Day, July 6, when small planes packed with rose petals flew low over our heads, scattering showers of petals along our red dancing lines as Bhagwan drove by.

Alas, the week was over all too soon. Most of us, about five thousand in all, had to leave, as in those days there was accommodation only for a few hundred residents on the Ranch. The rest of us had to go and find our way in the world.

Laurel Canyon

Reluctantly, I returned to LA, wondering what I was going to do with myself. I could always go back to the nightclub to earn money, but I missed being around my own people.

One day, while walking along Venice Beach, I met a sannyasin friend, Narayana, whom I had known working in the kitchen at the ashram in India. He was selling Indian jewelry and clothes on the sidewalk and invited me to come home with him.

Narayana was tall, blond, and good-looking. He had a great sense of humor and I loved to hear him talking in his imitation Hindi Bindi accent.

He had an old-style mala around his neck, meaning he had been with Bhagwan from the beginning. He didn't take this American show too seriously and it helped ease my trepidation.

He lived in a big house in Laurel Canyon, an area which had been a music hub for famous musicians in the late 1960s and early 1970s, including Frank Zappa, Joni Mitchell, Jim Morrison, Carole King, and others.

Narayana invited me to move in. The house had been home to The Monkees rock band. I used to watch those freewheeling boys every Saturday morning on TV in England, singing along with their upbeat songs:

"Hey, hey we're the Monkees, and people say we monkey around, but we're too busy singing, to put anybody down..."

In my bedroom in London, I used to swoon over lead singer Davy Jones, as his sweet voice sang out the song, "Daydream Believer." Now here I was, living in the very house where the Monkees had recorded those songs.

We were a motley crew of twenty adults, five kids, a large dog, and two cats. There were people living in every nook and cranny of the house, in the laundry room, in the treehouse, and in the large, converted garage. We were one big happy family.

Breakfast times were mayhem, with everyone scrambling to make food and eat. The kids would leave the kitchen in a chaos of mess with their pancake-making endeavors. We had to have someone constantly on kitchen duty just to keep the place clean and orderly.

Evening meals were more organized, with two adults responsible for cooking and serving dinner each day.

Sitting down to dinner with this large and rowdy family was a wild experience, and all the chores, the joys and sorrows were shared, as well as upsets and fights.

Some of us were rebels and free spirits but this little community also housed people who were rule keepers and order bringers, who constantly tried to whip us into shape. Impossible. We had tasted freedom, spontaneity and wildness in the Pune Ashram and were not about to give it up.

Tosh

It was in Laurel Canyon that I got together with Anutosh, an Englishman. "Tosh" was tall, regal, and handsome, with a Roman nose and a rascally twinkle in his green eyes.

Tosh had been an actor in London with the Royal Shakespeare Company and the National Theatre Company. He had given it all up to go and find himself with Bhagwan.

He had been a Samurai Guard in the Pune Ashram and was also an early resident on the Oregon Ranch, before finding those rough, pioneering days and long working hours a bit too much, and getting on the wrong side of Sheela and told to leave. Now he was here in Laurel Canyon.

I remember walking into the house for the first time, wearing my little 1950s consignment dress, looking suntanned—and cute and sexy I am sure—with little white shoes on my feet, and feeling kind of shy.

Tosh came straight up to me and said, "Hey darling, you're very pretty, aren't you? Wanna get together with me?"

I smiled coyly. I liked his cockiness, his ability to say whatever he felt. I allowed myself to be swept off my feet and it wasn't long before we ended up in bed together; our relationship took off from there. I was happy to have someone who could offer me an anchor.

Tosh was a rascal though and would take any drugs going around— cocaine, pot, and lots of alcohol.

When he got drunk, he would spout Shakespeare's wonderful musings and comic lines, asking deeper questions of man's existential experience.

Tosh could recite every line of every play by heart. I was always amazed by his ability to memorize lines, considering how many brain cells he was burning up with his prodigious consumption of drugs.

Fumbling towards Freedom / Rajyo Allen

Chapter Twenty
Wild Times Once Again

Those were the early days of a popular new drug called MDMA, also known as Ecstasy. In the early 1980s it was still legal, and we were guinea pigs for experimental batches being produced in Southern California.

For hours, we would lie naked by the fire on duvets spread on the floor, with Tosh holding court, spouting Shakespeare, and outrageously fondling the bodies of us women. The kids would come and serve us drinks and fruit and offer their captive audience plays and songs they had made up. Ecstasy, as most people know, was, and still is, a widely used party drug, and it was banned in 1985 by the US Drug Enforcement Administration. It offers a lovely high and feelings of heartfelt intimacy with other people, but with long term use it is tough on the body and makes brainwork foggy.

It was in that house that I also met Alima, also an English actress, who became my dearest spiritual friend. She and I recognized the soul longing in each other, and our deep sisterhood began then, living through all kinds of inner journeys and outer adventures, as we have been doing for forty years now. She has been a constant spiritual companion and fellow traveler in my life.

My Laurel Canyon era was marked by languid days lying naked by the pool in summer and cozy nights by a big open fire in winter. So, even here, in the city I had judged to be so heartless, my lifestyle became free and easy once more. I was with my soul tribe and family. We supported each other to live as we wished. It was after all, Laurel Canyon, and we were walking in the footsteps of the 1960s musicians, rebels, renegades, and creative artists who had themselves been on the outskirts of society. And that's how we were: living in the world and yet definitely not of the world, just as Bhagwan had recommended. We were grateful to have each other, as there was no way we were able to fit into the society surrounding us.

To make money, the men would do handyman work for house owners in LA, or sell jewelry, while the women did craft work which they sold at the local fairs and farmers markets.

Call Girl Initiation

To my surprise, a couple of women told me they worked as call girls. I was slightly shocked, but also intrigued.

The call girl money was very attractive, even more lucrative than when dancing in a nightclub. When I said I wanted to try it, I was introduced to Jennifer. She was well put together, LA-style, and had had several facelifts to keep up her immaculate image. She was our "madame" and would arrange appointments for us with businessmen, actors, and entrepreneurs; off we would go, sometimes to a hotel, occasionally to their homes. We might get a call at any time of the day or night and off we would go to a job.

I remember my first appointment. I was sent to an unfamiliar part of town, and I was glad Tosh was willing to drive me there in his big old 1950s car and wait for me. It was before cell phones, so I could not call him if anything happened. But it was reassuring, just knowing he was there, parked on the street outside, waiting for me.

I climbed the stairs in the apartment building, hesitated, then rang the doorbell. I didn't know what to expect. A well-dressed guy answered the door. He was a businessman. He seemed nice enough, but we didn't have too much to say to each other. He gave me a drink, but soon invited me to the bedroom where we took off our clothes. I could tell he just wanted to get off and I was to help him do that. I started fondling his penis and when he was aroused helped him come inside me. There was no thought about my pleasure, just what would satisfy him. I laid on top of him so I could feel in control, and also so that I could feel my own arousal, and pretty quickly he came inside me.

We laid together for five or ten minutes, not saying anything. Then I got up and got dressed. He paid me $500, which for less than an hour's work, felt like good money. I was relieved to meet Tosh in the car. He asked me how it was, and I shrugged and said "Okay," grateful that Tosh wasn't the jealous type. He leaned over and pulled me to him, whispering in my ear "It's just like shaking hands darling. Not a big deal!"

Blackouts and Boundaries

At other times, I would be called to go in the middle of the night to a party and be expected to socialize, drink, dance for, and sometimes have sex with, my client. On those occasions, to numb my anxiety, I would usually drink a lot of alcohol or snort cocaine.

Once, I remember waking up in bed next to a man and was not sure what had happened the evening before. It was a surreal experience that was to be repeated on several occasions and it was my good fortune that nothing serious or more harmful happened during these "blackouts."

Alima told me she could do this job like an acting role: she would put on the makeup and clothes, step into the call girl role, do the job, come home and be absolutely fine, stepping out of the role and back into herself and her life. It was harder for me. I was still young and impressionable, and I didn't have strong personal boundaries. All too often, especially in the beginning of my call girl career, making love with a strange man affected me more than I wished. Afterwards, I'd come home shaken and upset.

In LA, my clients were mostly lonely guys needing a quick fuck, or just longing for female company. Later, when I did the same thing in London, things were more interesting. As a high-end call girl, I would get to meet prominent people, such as

107

Lords and politicians. Sometimes, I was asked to do kinky stuff. Beneath that English, aristocratic stiff upper lip, lies a whole world of weirdness: tying people up, being tied up, slapping and whipping. Sado-masochistic stuff was never my thing, but for others it certainly was!

Power over Men

I enjoyed working as an exotic dancer most. It felt easy and natural to me, and the fact that I was slender and beautiful meant I could use my body to turn on men without having to have sex with them, which, of course, was preferable.

I remember being on stage and feeling very expanded energetically compared to the men I'd see sitting in the audience, victims of their own frustrated sexuality, somehow shrunken in their energy. I knew that dancing as a naked woman, offering my body while at the same time withholding it, gave me a strange power over them. I saw other women use and abuse that power. They danced in the club, but they hated the men and wanted to squeeze every bit of money from them that they could. For me, it was different. I felt love and compassion for these men, and even developed soft spots for the ones who would come in for genuine conversation and connection. I felt their loneliness and pain.

Sometimes I would also get off on sitting on their laps in my skimpy bathing suit, feeling their cock getting hard underneath me. Sometimes we would start moving together, and I'd feel their orgasm building and then the warm wet sensation in their pants as they came. Sometimes it disgusted me, at other times, I'd get off, too, and there would be a subtle sense of satisfaction to feel this secret connection we'd had in this dimly lit club atmosphere.

My work in the sex trade allowed me to see the subtle power women exert over men. Even though the modern feminist narrative is that men have been the ones subduing, suppressing, and abusing women for generations, and men have power over women, there's another side to the story that is little acknowledged. Women know how to control men, silently in the dark, and we often "stick it to them" in hateful revenge, shaming and blaming them, nagging, and criticizing them, humiliating and judging them, getting back at them for the pain we have endured. It's a two-way game, and neither side wins.

The Path to Bliss

Being in the sex business taught me a lot. In my experience, men will go anywhere and do anything for physical intimacy with a woman. They think that sex is the path to their bliss, but there's something else they're looking for that sadly they miss.

The whole world is at a tragic loss because women never really get to share their own true power and beauty, and men never get to receive that. Everyone misses the mark, and all kinds of perversions develop out of this. Bhagwan used to say that what people think of as "normal sex" is just using the other person's body as an object to satisfy and release our urges. We do not really see or respect the other human being.

He taught that, deep down, our longing is not for sex. Sex is a doorway, but it's not the experience that's available in the temple. If you go through the doorway, you have access to something larger, more fulfilling.

Men tend to think, "If I can just get together with that cute chick, or that gorgeous woman, even for a night, that's going to be so fantastic!" But it's not. Or, let's say, it actually happens and does turn out to be a wonderful experience, but still, that's not going to last, not at that level of intensity, because the attraction is only surface-to-surface, image to image, body to body. It doesn't go any deeper.

I was struck the first time I heard the Australian Tantra guru, Barry Long, talking about women's deep frustration and rage, which he labelled "The Fiendess." He said that women are longing to offer men their deepest most secret feminine essence, but because we have been conditioned to have sex in

109

the most basic and unconscious way, women never get to share that sweet nectar with men. So, men and women settle for temporary sexual release, but neither gets truly replenished and nourished by the feminine energy, or Shakti, that is available.

As a result, unfulfilled male power is finding other expressions, in violence, in greed, in hunger for power, in mindless competition with each other.

I feel grateful that around Bhagwan I had an experience of sex being freely given and freely received, naturally, abundantly, with no rules, roles, or limits. It has been a great blessing in my life to live my sexuality fully and to experience it as a doorway to deeper layers of my being.

Chapter Twenty-One
The Ranch

By the end of his time on the Ranch, Bhagwan's collection of Rolls-Royces had risen to a grand total of ninety-three.

In a way, he seemed to be saying, "Look world. This is where you have your attention. In the wrong place. On accumulating stuff, like fancy cars, and yet you are so poor in spirit."

There was a strong PR element in Bhagwan's glamourous collection of glitzy automobiles. "Without those Rolls-Royces nobody would be interested in what is happening here," he told one visiting journalist.

Personally, I couldn't care less about the cars. I loved him because what he said about humans and their spiritual quest made sense to me. He spoke a truth that resonated deep in my heart, and I was thankful every day to be part of this huge experiment that had begun in Pune and was now exploding in Oregon. I remember the energy generated around the world when sannyasins started realizing Bhagwan was in Oregon, and that we were building a city where we all could live and flourish. We were so excited, and desperate to be there with the Master.

There was a lot of travel to and from the Ranch, first to the massive summer festival and then, as the infrastructure grew and more and more houses were built, hundreds of people started to live there. Sannyasins from around the world were welcomed to the Ranch, including the stragglers and strays, like me, who were not sure where we belonged, but knew we wanted to be close to Bhagwan.

America was a strange and foreign place, but on the Ranch, we were happy to see our brothers and sisters, who had by now exchanged their flowing saffron robes for red jeans, maroon t-shirts, and the occasional cowboy hat.

Humming in the Hive

Friends, even women, were driving dump trucks, bulldozers, backhoes, and all kinds of construction equipment. Others worked in offices, restaurants, cafeterias, out on the farm, in the garage, and in woodworking and metalworking shops.

I was given the green light to move to the commune and found we were like busy little worker bees, humming in the hive. Gone were the days of doing Dynamic Meditation as the sun rose over the lush gardens of the Pune ashram, with exotic birds serenading in a new day. Gone, also, was the lazy rhythm of drifting through the day with little or no schedule, dropping in for a meditation in Buddha Hall, hanging out in the ashram, drinking chai, slipping off to make love with a beautiful lover. It was a heavenly existence and India addicts like me wanted to spend the rest of our days that way.

At the Ranch, our days were very different. We were up before daylight and off to the canteens for breakfast; then we gathered at our workplaces to meditate and offer our devotion through a beautiful, haunting chant taken from the Buddhist tradition:

Buddham Saranam Gacchami

Dhammam Saranam Gacchami

Sangham Saranam Gacchami

Meaning:

I take refuge in the Awakened One,

I take refuge in the Ultimate Truth of the Awakened One,

I take refuge in the Commune of the Awakened One.

For me, as for most of us, this was a gesture of surrendering our individual will to the greater vision of an enlightened Master, and thereby setting the scene for a day of hard work and lots of fun. No matter what we did as sannyasins, there was always a lot of lightness and laughter.

Commune Life

I worked in the large cafeteria, called "Magdalena," where everyone would gather to eat breakfast, lunch, and dinner each day. It was the hub of community life, so different from Vindravan, the small intimate kitchen in the ashram in India, where I had worked before.

There were huge pots boiling on big commercial stoves and massive amounts of food prepared for each meal to feed hundreds of people. The population increased to many thousands when we held festivals, so massive amounts of food were always being made. Veggie chopping, cooking, baking, and washing up all happened here, so it was a lively place.

I had many jobs in Magdalena, but most of all I loved working in the bakery. That involved getting up in the wee hours of the morning to get to the bakery, where we would knead dough and bake the pastries that were a yummy treat for the hungry crews. The early shift was an intimate crew, with just three or four of us, all covered in flour, cracking jokes and baking bread and pastries. There was no place I would rather be.

At the end of each day, everything would stop, and the whole place would be scrubbed from top to bottom. They say that cleanliness is next to Godliness. If so, we must have been pretty darn close to God. There was so much to do, but it was always relaxing at the end of the day to sit together with my friends, and rest our weary bodies. We would drink chai, joke, and laugh, and somehow there was always enough energy to go to the disco, to dance and flirt, and occasionally to have a flutter at the gambling tables, and even then, if a lover came along, another burst of energy would carry us home together.

Endless Waves of Energy

Our energy seemed unlimited. Just when we thought we were done, another surge would carry us forward. It was unbelievable what we could, and did, achieve in those Oregon years. We built a town for 3,500 people in four years and had a great time doing it. There was never a dull moment. One day, I was told to leave Magdalena and join a female construction crew because there was a rush to build fifty-two townhouses before a building moratorium was imposed by county officials. My roofing sisters and I would spend the day hammering in tiles and shingles, while gossiping among ourselves and eyeing the sexy-looking male construction workers below us as they strode around with tool belts slung around their hips like cowboys in old Western movies.

I had little knowledge of the conflict that was brewing outside the Ranch, beyond the fact that we seemed to be facing increasing opposition from Christian fundamentalists, redneck ranchers, land use groups, and county and state politicians. But once in a while, this other reality poked its nose into my life.

"Rajyo, this morning, we need to make separate food for the deposition team," I was told by one of the kitchen bosses.

"Huh? What's a deposition?" I'd never heard the term before.

"Legal stuff. Interviews for court cases."

"Okay, sure."

Much more interesting for me were the grand festivals, such as on March 21st, Bhagwan's Enlightenment Day, and July 6th, Master's Day. Thousands of people who could not live full time at the Ranch flew in from Europe, Latin America, Australia, and Japan, to be together with Bhagwan and celebrate.

Huge tent cities would appear to accommodate everyone, and for a week we would enjoy an international sannyasin love fest, laughing, playing, and connecting with old and new friends from every corner of the globe. Work would be put on hold for the week, and we'd simply enjoy each other's company, as well as sit in silence every day with Bhagwan in the Ranch's enormous open-sided meditation hall called Rajneesh Mandir.

After lunch, we would line up along the roads as Bhagwan drove slowly by, smiling and laughing, waving his arms in time to the music from our improvised roadside bands, and somehow managing to steer his car at the same time.

Chapter Twenty-Two
The Dream Unravels

But even here on the Ranch, in our beloved utopian city, things started changing.

I remember being at lunch in one of the dining tents during a festival, talking with friends. At a certain point, the tone of their voices lowered as they whispered to me about the group of women who were in charge, doing strange things.

It was disturbing when I heard that certain friends had been told to leave the Ranch, mysteriously and without warning. There was an air of suspicion and secrecy in the air, and I got the feeling it wasn't good to know too much. I guess I began to bury my head in the sand, hanging on to the good old days of innocence and wonder.

Bhagwan had stopped giving discourses before leaving India, and his public silence continued on the Ranch for the first two or three years. As I mentioned earlier, he had appointed a young Gujarati woman named Sheela as his secretary, replacing Laxmi, and she met with Bhagwan every day at his house for a private talk. We believed that her commands were coming directly from Bhagwan, which was mainly true.

But, as we found out later, Sheela was also pursuing her own private agenda. She was running the day-to-day business of the Ranch from a compound called Jesus Grove, located in the center of the main valley. She and her select group of managers made this their central hub, and you could be called there, without notice, to be hired or fired from a job, told to leave the Ranch, or given an unexpected promotion.

Much later, after Sheela had left, we learned of even stranger goings on: wiretapping of the buildings so people could spy on us, and bizarre plots to "bump off" members of Bhagwan's personal staff, of whom Sheela was jealous. For example, one of the crimes to which Sheela eventually pleaded guilty in an American court was the attempted murder of Bhagwan's personal doctor, an English sannyasin called Amrito.

AIDS

In the Spring of 1984, Bhagwan warned that AIDS, a new and mysterious disease, which up to that time seemed to be confined to America's gay community and drug addicts using contaminated needles, would become a worldwide epidemic, spreading rapidly through the heterosexual population. He sent a message via Sheela, telling us to use latex gloves during foreplay, condoms during sex and he also banned kissing.

I pretty much stopped making love at that point, because it was all too funny, trying to make love, covered in rubber gloves and condoms, but without kissing. I found it hysterical. When testing for AIDS became possible, a distant trailor complex was set up for half-a-dozen Ranch residents who showed up as HIV positiv. My friend Zeno, a lively, irreverent Jewish American woman was sent there, but I later learned she'd discovered information about Sheela's illegal activities and was sent there to keep her quiet. She didn't have the HIV virus.

One day, I was called to the Ranch medical center. My eyes were examined and I was told I had conjunctivitis. I was sent to a large A-frame complex in a narrow canyon off the Ranch's main valley and was soon joined there by many friends. They kept coming until almost the whole work force was there, in quarantine. We kept checking each other for symptoms of redness, itchiness, pain, but nothing was apparent. We thought it was weird, but were glad to have a few days off work, where we could just hang out with each other. I found out later that this was when a lot of bugging devices were installed for wiretapping, especially in Bhagwan's personal compound, allowing Sheela to eavesdrop on peoples' conversations.

Sheela's increasing paranoia was partly understandable given the increasing hostility being directed at our community from outside. In response, she was talking tough on local TV stations and later claimed that Bhagwan had told her to rabble-rouse, but since Bhagwan wasn't giving discourses, we had no idea what part, if any, he played in the unfolding of the drama.

Street People

More drama was to come. In a bid to take over Wasco County, where the Ranch was located, the Ranch managers sent out recruiting teams to cities across the United States to invite surprised homeless people to come live with us. Suddenly, there were bewildered homeless men and women arriving, with no idea why they were invited, but happy to be given good food and warm shelter. We hid all the knives and cleaning supplies, but still, the Ranch felt unsafe after they arrived. As it turned out, some of these people did end up falling in love with Bhagwan and staying until the very end, but for most it was just a free meal and an interesting diversion from street life. Sheela's plan was to have these characters vote in the November 1984 elections, but the county saw through her tactic and barred any new voter registration so the ruse failed. Soon afterwards, these street people were bussed back to where they had come from—back to their lives on America's streets.

Sheela Leaves the Ranch

I was not on the Ranch when things started to unravel. In September 1985, while I was back in San Francisco, dancing to make money to return to Oregon, I heard that Sheela and her closest associates—the ones involved in criminal activity—had left the Ranch and flown to Switzerland.

As soon as Sheela left, sannyasins who had been working with her came forward with a list of crimes in which she had been involved. Bhagwan surprised us all by going public with it in discourse and then invited the local police to investigate. Meanwhile, Bhagwan himself was facing a determined effort by President Ronald Reagan and his administration to have him deported, with the idea that if he could be thrown out of the country, the Ranch would collapse.

As tension reached the boiling point, there were rumors that the Ranch was about to be invaded by hundreds of armed police and SWAT teams, aimed at arresting Bhagwan at gunpoint. Attempts to negotiate a peaceful surrender were rebutted by the US Attorney for Oregon, Charles Turner.

Bhagwan's Arrest

Late one afternoon, Bhagwan boarded a private jet with his closest devotees and headed for the Bahamas. The plane got as far as Charlotte, North Carolina, before it was grounded and he was arrested. It was heartbreaking to see my Master on the television news, his beautiful delicate hands in handcuffs, as he was taken into custody and transported from jail to the courthouse. I couldn't believe what was happening. How had things gone so terribly wrong? My heart ached to see this small, frail Indian man, with his beautiful long white hair and beard, locked up and held in prison for many days.

During this time his lawyers did not know where he was and we later heard that the government had administered thallium poisoning, which is undetectable but deadly and which would destroy Bhagwan's health eventually. He was finally sent back to Portland for trial. Bhagwan had mocked the political systems of this world with all its hypocrisy and injustice. Now he himself was being subjected to it. His lawyers agreed to a plea bargain, he was charged with immigration fraud and entered an Alford plea, not admitting guilt but agreeing there was evidence that could convict him.

Bhagwan was fined $400,000 and immediately deported from the US. From there, he travelled with his little entourage around the world, trying to find a place to create a new community. He went to twenty-one countries, from Greece to Uruguay, but due to pressure from the US Government, he was never allowed to remain in one place very long. Eventually, he had no choice but to return to his native India. Without Osho as its magnet, the Ranch could not sustain itself economically and soon we were all being asked to leave. Once again, we turned our backs on paradise and faced an uncertain future in the world.

Chapter Twenty-Three
Back in the World

As the Ranch ended, our community of sannyasins disbanded and dispersed. I went to live with a bunch of friends in a communal house in Marin County, just north of San Francisco, and we tried as best we could to support each other.

My basic income came from dancing at the Mitchell Brothers Theater on O'Farrell Street, San Francisco, which was by now famous throughout America for its onstage strip shows combined with "lap dancing" by scantily clad women who moved around the audience, sitting on men's laps, and making out with them for cash. No actual sex was allowed, but, as I mentioned earlier, it was easy to turn on these sex-starved guys through their clothing—providing they were ready to open their wallets. In an effort to numb the pain of what had happened in Oregon, many of us slipped back into using drugs and alcohol. Our lives on the Ranch had been brutally disrupted and we felt lost, so it was somehow inevitable to seek refuge in old habits. I was twenty-five years old at this time, still very much trying to find my way in the world, still very influenced by others, and I did not have a clue what my own path might look like.

Reconnecting with Tosh

I went to Santa Fe to meet up with Tosh, who, all this time, had been doing his best to woo me off the Ranch, sending drunken tapes of him singing love songs to me. Of course, true to his nature, a wild time was on offer, and I found the same thing happening there as in Marin: lots of drugs and debauchery. He and I went on to Rio de Janeiro, where we lived for a while with old friends from Laurel Canyon. We stayed there for six months, enjoying the Brazilian lifestyle, especially during

Carnival time. But late nights and alcohol were not quenching the thirst I felt for a deeper spiritual context for my life. I left Tosh in Brazil and flew back to Santa Fe, where I had an intense love affair with a sannyasin man who claimed he was into Tantra and Zen. His version of this combination was to make passionate love for hours and then stop and sit in meditation, using our aroused energies to intensify an inner sense of spiritual expansion.

But this was not my cup of tea. It seemed too contrived and mechanical, and although the sexual attraction between us was strong it lacked any deep heart connection, which for me was so important in any love affair.

I flew back to San Francisco where I met up with Tosh again and lived with him in the city's Castro District, famous for its gay scene and permissive lifestyle. Tosh, the old rascal, succeeded in recapturing my heart. But, alas, not for long. I was getting tired of his drinking and compulsive flirting with other women. It might have been enough for him, but for me it did nothing to fill the aching hole left by Bhagwan's departure and the collapse of the Ranch.

The final straw came one night when Tosh staggered into our apartment, accompanied by a young woman who was also "out of it" on drugs or alcohol, dressed in a faded t-shirt and cutoff jeans. She smiled weakly at me.

"What's going on, Tosh?" I asked, impatiently. It was late and I was already heading for bed.

"She's a hooker I met on the street outside," he slurred, drunkenly. "She doesn't have anywhere to sleep tonight. I thought maybe she could share our bed."

"What? Tosh, are you out of your mind? No way!"

Enough was enough! I sighed heavily and saw her out the door and locked it. This incident happened right after I'd caught Tosh stealing money from my bag to buy cocaine. We broke up and this time I knew it was final. But I couldn't help chuckling to myself when I thought of us all trying to get some sleep after a long night of cocaine, and Tosh would not stop talking.

"Shut up, Tosh!" we would plead. "Well then, pay me!" he would retort, "a dollar a minute." He made some serious money that night.

My Next Lover

Even though I had enjoyed affairs with many lovers, I was still young and always hoping that the next man in my life would be "the one" with whom I could melt, merge, and find lasting fulfillment. Sure enough, it wasn't long before the next candidate showed up.

Rupesh, a slightly crazy Mexican sannyasin who was a passionate drummer, and who had played tablas and bongos for Bhagwan, introduced me to another musician, who was also a drummer, and also Mexican. I will call him "Miguel" to shield his identity. This guy was very sexy, with big "come-to-bed-with-me" eyes and "kiss-me" lips, and a body that turned me on like crazy. We danced well together, especially in bed. Enthusiastically, I launched myself headlong into another relationship. We lived together in California and also in the Mexican Caribbean, where for a short time we helped run a retreat center on the beach in Tulum, living an idyllic lifestyle

In 1987, when Bhagwan returned to the Pune ashram, at the end of the mystic's world tour, I wanted to be with my Master once more and took Miguel with me. Of course, I knew very well this might jeopardize our love affair, given the "free love" atmosphere, but the pull to be with Bhagwan was too strong and I had to go. Naturally, Miguel fell in love with Bhagwan and was soon invited to join the band of musicians who played at the beginning and end of the Master's discourses. Miguel was thrilled. It also made him very popular, and he quickly started flirting with several of the gorgeous women now pouring into the ashram. For the first time, I was consumed with jealousy, which, as every woman knows, is one of the worst feelings a lover can have—that awful wrenching inside your guts when you feel the man you love is focusing his attention and sexual energy elsewhere. As Barry Long might have put it, Miguel brought out "the fiendess" in me. "You're mine! MINE!" I wanted to scream.

Jealousy and Beyond

I decided I would show him how jealousy felt. I got together with an Italian sannyasin and spent a hot night with him. When I told Miguel about it the next day, he was furious with me, not just because I had slept with another man, but because I had spoiled the "high" he had derived from playing for the Master that night. After that, Miguel felt he had permission to sleep with whomever he liked. He got together with a luscious Italian woman and soon she and I were in competition. But I did succeed in going beyond my jealousy. On our last night in Pune, I suggested the three of us get together, and we did. I can still hear his Italian lover moaning "Mio Dio!" calling out for God as she climaxed. I felt no jealousy, only joy that I could share this experience of making love with the man I loved, as he made love to another woman. Somehow it brought Miguel and I closer together and we made out in the taxi on the way to the airport.

Back in California, Miguel and I lived in a large house in Mill Valley with several other sannyasins who were mostly musicians. Once again, I found myself in a mad whirl of music, chaos, and laughter, with no rules. I was very much in love with Miguel but could never relax because I was always afraid he was never fully committed to me. I couldn't trust that he really loved me—he was such a ladies' man. I started using cocaine to escape the anxiety and pain. All night, I would stay up snorting and smoking. Late in the morning, I would drag myself out of bed, then go to work in the afternoon, dancing at Mitchell Brothers in San Francisco. I would have to snort another line of cocaine to keep me awake and I'd wash it down with a glass of orange juice and spirulina for sustenance. It was no life at all, and I was on a fast track to ruin. I was miserably unhappy and dangerously thin. Once again, I started to look like a skeleton.

Changing My Ways

When my best friend Alima came visiting from Hawaii, she looked shocked. "My God, Chinny, you look terrible!" She always called me Chinny, which in Hindi means "sugar." Trust your bestie to tell you the truth!

"What are you doing to yourself?" Ali almost shook me, in her effort to get me to realize my poor condition. "You need to get away from here. You need to get well and put on some weight. Come to Hawaii and be with the girls."

I didn't need much convincing. I left Miguel and the boys to have their fun, thinking, "They probably won't miss me, anyway."

Once again, I had been looking for love in all the wrong places. I needed to come back to myself. Being in Hawaii with my girlfriends was a welcome relief. The warm sunshine, the balmy ocean and the warmth and genuine love of Alima and other dear friends, soothed my aching heart and exhausted body.

I went through a withdrawal period as I gave up cigarettes, alcohol, cocaine, and all other drugs, and finally began to put on weight. I was twenty-eight and this was the moment in astrology known as my "Saturn return." Saturn takes twenty-eight years to make one revolution around the sun, so it was the time when Saturn returned to the position where it had been at my birth. According to astrology, Saturn return allows the qualities of this planet, such as maturity, wisdom, and discipline, to support an individual to make important life changes. In my case, it was clearly time to change my ways and get my life together. When I returned to California, I broke up with Miguel, and we went our separate ways. My way, naturally enough, led me back to India.

Fumbling towards Freedom / Rajyo Allen

Chapter Twenty-Four
Return to India

When Bhagwan drove in through the gates of the ashram in Pune again, early in 1987, the ashram that had been dormant, gathering dust during our Oregon years, began to flourish once more. People flooded in from all parts of the globe and we were so glad to meet old friends whom we hadn't seen for so long.

On the Ranch, it had been work, work, work, with little time for hanging out. Now, back in the land of buddhas and enlightened beings, there was plenty of time for meditation, ease, and playfulness, for love and lightness and joy.

Doing Dynamic Meditation in Buddha Hall reminded me of the old days, feeling the ecstasy of moving beyond all limits within myself, surrounded by hundreds of other mad fools who were also hungry for God. Afterwards, I would sit on the marble walkway around the periphery of Buddha Hall, in the cool shade of bamboos and flowering trees to eat my breakfast and listen to Bhagwan's discourse—which was played every morning on audiotape inside the hall—while exotic birds sang in the branches above my head.

Life was once again simple and beautiful. Even though Bhagwan had originally left Pune because we needed a larger place, necessity proved to be the mother of invention, and the ashram now responded to our need by growing exponentially. The management bought several adjacent buildings, built new ones, and added extra space wherever it could. Magnificent pyramid-shaped buildings went up and, according to Bhagwan's wishes, everything was painted black, giving the ashram buildings an austere Zen beauty. It was a different time, not as intimate as my first Pune experience, but definitely more gentle, loving, and relaxed than the Ranch had been. Here, we had time to meditate again, to allow the luxury of living around the Master, and to respond to the calling of the moment.

From Bhagwan to Osho

Bhagwan changed his name to "Osho," which is a Japanese term of reverence for a spiritual teacher. He pointed out that "Osho" sounds like "ocean," and this pleased him because, as he explained, disappearing into the inner emptiness is an oceanic experience. Osho was back to giving daily discourses and had a lot to say about what had happened in Oregon. He spoke about the corruption of American politicians and their efforts to destroy the Ranch. He condemned Sheela for her deeds and for misusing the power she derived from her position as his secretary.

As a Master, he never gave us ten commandments about what to do and not do. But he did teach awareness and the opportunity to learn through life experience, and that went deep.

When I think about it now, I see how I had to navigate the tricky worlds of religion and politics which, unfortunately, are rife with people trying to manipulate the innocence and trust of others. When I think back on it, wow, that was a great lesson. It made me so much more aware of the corruption going on in our world, and more able to trust my own inner guidance and follow my own truth. That lesson, although painful, has been priceless.

Death Celebration

For the next three years, I went back and forth between Pune and California, spending as much time in India in the winter as I could, before the soaring temperatures of the hot season drove me out around March each year. With the end of 1989 and the beginning of another New Year, the time came when I usually departed for the East, but this time I decided I was not going. I had a feeling to stay home and focus on my life and work as a massage therapist, so it was a real shock when, on January 19, 1990, I heard from friends that Osho had died.

I felt bewildered. How could this be? How could he suddenly not be here? I could not believe I would never see him again. Enviously, I thought of the huge death celebration that must be happening in Pune, which I was going to miss. Even if I flew out on the next plane, it would be too late and I would miss the "Mahasamadhi," the liberation from the body of my Beloved Master, Osho.

Whenever someone died in the ashram, they were laid out on a dais in the main hall for all to see, the body covered in flowers, while sannyasins danced and sang all around, raising the energy to give him or her a good send-off.

Then the body would be carried in a colorful procession, with lots of singing, drumming and firecrackers, down to the burning ghats by the river, about half a kilometer's distance. There, the body would be laid on wooden logs, then covered with more logs, and set alight.

I knew that with Osho there would be an even bigger celebration, honoring the fact that he was now liberated from the restrictions of the form, and his soul was free to fly into the infinite sky. Two days later, his ashes were brought back to the ashram in a brass urn and laid to rest in a white marble 'Samadhi' in Chuang Tzu Auditorium.

About a year earlier, at Osho's request, the old auditorium had been enclosed with green-tinted glass panels, running from floor to ceiling, and it had been tiled with Italian white marble. Ostensibly, this was because Osho wanted a new bedroom, but we eventually realized, after his death, that he was actually creating the mausoleum where his ashes would lie. He had spent just a few nights sleeping there before returning to his old room.

Even though I missed the celebration, I flew to India as soon as I could. I wanted to be with my friends and feel the fragrance of our crazy mystic Master. Paradoxically, when I walked in the gate, the energy in the ashram seemed even higher after his death.

A Magnet for Us

Osho had been the magnet that had drawn us all together. He was the glue that held us firmly in the heart of his Buddhafield. He was the source of love that we had come to know and share with each other. He was the provider of the vision that we lived so fully and intensely. What an immense gift he had given us.

Osho said that when he died, he would live on in his sannyasins and there is a certain truth to it. Whenever we look into each other's eyes, no matter where in the world we are, and no matter how long since we have seen each other, there is a bright spark of recognition and love.

Sannyasins have a world wide web of connection through our love for Osho and his vision for the New Man, which he called "Zorba the Buddha."

He wanted us to live fully *in* the world, just like Zorba did, living and playing fully with Life, but not be *of* the world; to be so steeped in meditative awareness that we also carry the fragrance of the Buddha.

We know what we have shared: living communally, building a vision, journeying together, baring our souls, working on ourselves, laughing, playing, diving deep, simply being with each other, in love with life and free to follow our hearts. Osho's gift remains with us always.

Chapter Twenty-Five
Lessons in Love

"Where in the world do I want to be?"

It was my own existential question. After Osho died, India continued to be the home of my heart, but I felt adrift, because my main reason for being there had gone.

For a while, I continued traveling between India, California, and Europe. I didn't know where I wanted to settle, but I ended up in California with a bunch of old friends, and we lived communally together. We set about looking for property to purchase to continue living this way, but there was nothing around the Northern California area we could afford.

Alima and some other close friends eventually went to Australia and found affordable land there in a beautiful rainforest on the East Coast, just outside Byron Bay.

I was planning to emigrate to Australia also, but hesitated because I had a boyfriend, a young Thai-German sannyasin, named Kumar. We met in the ashram on Valentine's Day when he was nineteen and I was thirty-one.

With our first kiss, I fell completely in love with him. He was such an enigma to me: he had exotic eyes, a sexy German-English accent, smooth olive skin and a lithe Asian body that really turned me on. His long dark hair would flow over the pillow as we lay together, making love on cool sheets, with him staying inside me for hours, gazing into each other's eyes, our bodies melting into bliss in a deep valley orgasm.

Making love with him was an endless melting into oneness: there were not two of us, we were like one being. I had never before experienced this degree of union with a lover.

Kumar and I enjoyed many wild adventures and much laughter together. I loved to ride on his motorbike from Pune to Goa, enjoying the deep hum of the engine beneath us as we cruised through the countryside and dodged the crazy Indian vehicles that have no road safety rules whatsoever.

I was fascinated by his depth and intensity, the way he dove into courses—such as the ashram's Tantra Training and its Rebalancing Bodywork Training—at such a young age.

A Mystery to Me

He was an amazing bodyworker, and I loved the way his hands always knew how to touch me, heal me, and turn me on. He was playful and passionate, older than his years. A Cancer sun sign, he was sensitive and soulful.

Sometimes he would disappear into his shell, and I would not be able to reach him. Those were lonely times for me, and I just had to wait until he was ready to re-emerge. My little Asian Prince, Kumar, was a mystery to me.

Aside from our travels around India, we also ventured through Nepal, Thailand, and Europe.

We finally settled in England at the sannyasin school, Ko Hsuan, in Devon, where I taught dance and yoga and Kumar taught photography. I was happy to be back in the womb-like atmosphere of communal life. It was alive and juicy to be with kids of all ages, from five right through to graduation age. They were savvy, smart, and fun to be with.

I became close with several of the teenage girls, and it was healing for my own inner teenager to be met by these wild and wise young divas, all older than their years. The boys were also intelligent and emotionally available, and I couldn't help but see Bhagwan's vision unfolding in these evolved souls. The

New Man he talked about was coming alive in these young hearts.

At Ko Hsuan, every child, even the youngest, were responsible for doing their schoolwork, but also had to share in duties of cooking and cleaning.

Everyone attended house meetings where decisions were made, and in addition to learning, having fun, and playing, each person knew they had a say in how the school was run.

This was what I loved about Kumar. Having grown up in Ko Hsuan himself, he had a beautiful balance of maturity, sincerity, and deep presence. He could be like a spontaneous child, a free spirit, and an old soul all at once, a combination that seemed to offer the deepest intimacy I had ever experienced.

So, as you can imagine, I was taken by surprise one day when he picked me up at the station upon my return from London and, walking me home to the school, he turned to me with sad solemn eyes and said, "I need to go. I need to end our relationship. I need to find my freedom and explore the world on my own."

"Whaaaat?" I shrieked as I burst into tears. I could not believe what my ears were hearing. We kept walking, but I was not there. My mind kept wondering what I had done wrong that could have made him decide to leave.

When we entered the cute country bedroom in the cottage we shared, the low attic ceiling seemed to cave in on me. The windows seemed to imprison me in an impossible reality.

I had loved this room in which we had shared such a magical romance. It had been our haven from the world. I sat on the bed and looked at all the love notes pinned to the walls, sweet silly love notes that now felt so shallow and empty.

Maybe I had been fooling myself. Perhaps he never meant any of it. Perhaps it was all a dream and now I had to wake up and live my life, alone, without my dream lover, Kumar.

Hollow Inside

Now it was over. I was hollow inside. I couldn't face life or the world. That old, old wound of being left by my mother opened up and I felt like my life was over.

Even though it was warm and sunny outside, I was shivering uncontrollably, as that old abandonment wound resurfaced.

I watched him pick up his bags, which were already packed. His mind was made up. I could have spent the rest of my life beside this beautiful being, but he was too young to settle in a permanent relationship.

He had so much to live and experience – things I had already seen and done. The age difference between us was showing now, whereas before it hadn't mattered at all.

Weakly, I did my best to let him go, while inwardly screaming for him to stay. I said to him, "I hear you. I love you. I have been loving settling down with you, and I so wish you wanted that too. I guess you need to go. I will miss you so much."

I could see by the sad look he returned to me that he could feel the pain he was causing me. He didn't want to get too close, for fear of losing himself in me.

I could feel him pulling away. The symbiotic space we had shared, was over now. His heart was leaving me.

"I'm sorry to hurt you. I hope you're gonna be okay," he said.

We held each other for a long time. For the last time.

Then, he pulled away and I watched him walk out the bedroom door. I heard him walk down the stairs and shut the cottage door behind him.

I knew he was never coming back. It was final. I was alone once more.

Chapter Twenty-Six
Shattered

I cried like I had never cried before. I could not believe Kumar was gone. It was all over. Like a dream. No long, drawn-out separation drama, no bargaining, just a clear, simple goodbye. My heart was shattered into a thousand pieces. I could not imagine life without him. I stayed in that room for the weekend, crying an ocean of tears, for my love, for my life, for what we had shared and what would never be again.

I wondered what I had done to cause him to leave. Was it the affair I had had in Pune with the tall burly German guy who had roused my passion, and with whom I had spent a few hot nights? Up until that time, Kumar and I had been in an innocent state of blissful love. Maybe that had caused him to begin to close his heart to me. Damn, damn, damn! Why was I such a slave to my hormones, to impulse and sexual attraction! Why did I do such a stupid thing to the man I loved?

I could not face going back to the school, with the kids asking me, "Where is Kumar?" Maybe they already knew, maybe he had told them he was leaving before he told me. A deep sense of shame made me want to disappear into a hole in the ground and never come out. Was there something wrong with me? It reminded me of not being told of my mother's death. What did everyone else know that I didn't? I felt small, lonely, and cold, without the warm blanket of Kumar's love enveloping me.

I went to London to take refuge in my father's embrace while pouring out my troubles to him. From there, I went to California, but I could not find my place there. I got on a plane to Australia to be with my friends in Byron Bay and heal my

133

broken heart. I knew that with Alima and other old pals I could at least relax, let go, and be my messy, miserable self.

Healing in the Sunshine

It took many months for my heart to heal and to regain some joy in life, but the warm Australian sunshine, the beaches, and the ocean—as well as lots of laughter with my irreverent friends—slowly helped me recover. With them, I could begin to release the dream I had woven with Kumar. Yes, those experiences of melting into oneness had been real, but they were fleeting. And the assumption of togetherness and permanence that had blossomed in my heart out of those experiences, well, I was being shown not to hold onto them or I would suffer.

"Love is blind." I remembered that old saying and it astonished me how true it could be, even for those of us on a spiritual path, aspiring to self-knowledge and awareness. It stunned me that such incredibly beautiful experiences could go hand in hand with such abandonment and pain. That was the real mystery of my time with Kumar.

But life, love, and romance weren't done with me yet. At thirty-three? No, not at all. While I was hanging out with my friends in the rain forest, I met up with Rohit, a spritely, sun-bronzed, red-headed Australian sannyasin whom I had first met in Pune. He was a year older than me and a great tennis player, with that sporty, outdoor, Aussie vibe. We started to hang out together, and when we hugged and kissed for the first time at a party, I enjoyed the feeling of his strong arms around me. It felt good to be held like that.

He smiled. "Wanna come home with me?"

"Sure," I said, feeling more than ready for some tender loving. I felt shy, uncertain if I wanted to open up to a man again, but he was in no hurry, and that suited me fine. I knew this was a rebound relationship, as I was busy trying to fill the hole in my heart that Kumar had left.

Rohit and I had a good time together, riding on his motorbike, having fun on the beaches, surfing in the waves. He was sweet, gentle, and good to be around. I appreciated our conversations and his innocent heart, and I knew he cared about me. I had a feeling with Rohit that everything was right there, on the surface, simple and easy, with none of the mystery of having to figure out what was going on, as I had done with Kumar.

A New Life

We dated for several months, enjoying the energy flowing between us. One night, after a party, as we sat quietly around a fire outside, I looked at the reflection of the burning fire on his face, and felt my heart quicken with an intimate passion. He must have felt it, too, because he leaned over to me and whispered in my ear.

"I'd like to spend more time with you, and travel with you" he said. "Shall we go on an adventure together?"

I noticed something bubbling up inside me and it felt good to have someone want me. I felt a sudden surge of love for him in my heart, and a subtle 'yes', moved inside me.

You must surely be shaking your head at this point in my tale, as I seem to be staggering from one guy to the next, seeking something elusive. In my defense, I can only say that, for once, I wanted to experience a love that felt solid and grounded. All the cards were on the table, so to speak. I was done with delusions, fantasies, and painful surprises. Here was a guy I could trust. I knew he wasn't the love of my life, and I knew in my heart it was a rebound relationship, I longed to begin to open up to someone with whom I could create a future. To live in Australia with Rohit and be close to my friends and start a new life here felt good. After several months in Australia, we went to England to meet my dad.

We were married in the Chelsea Registry office on King's Road, the trendy shopping street where my family had lived when I was a toddler. It was a simple ceremony, with a few friends, including Tosh, followed by a celebration at my father's Chelsea flat.

On our way back to Australia, we decided to make a stopover in India for a honeymoon. I wanted to show Rohit the Himalayas. We went to Manali, which was magical for both of us, and the cool mountain air made me feel happy and alive. While we were there, Rohit decided he wanted to ride a motorbike to Nepal. This created a problem. I didn't want to ride on the back of his bike for such a long trip, as I feared it would bring up too many old memories of similar adventures in India with Kumar.

Clearly, my heart had not yet fully healed. So, I stayed in the mountains with friends who lived in the apple orchards overlooking Manali, while Rohit jumped on his big bike and roared off into the sunset. I did not hear from him for a while and began to get concerned. Finally, I heard from friends that he had had an accident, hit his head, and suffered concussion. I was extremely worried about him, as in those days few people on the Indian subcontinent wore helmets and everyone drove like maniacs, disregarding any road safety rules.

To my relief, Rohit faxed a message to me, saying he was fine. I wanted to join him in Nepal, but he told me not to come, and that we would see each other soon. I anxiously awaited his return, but weeks passed and still he didn't come.

The next news came as a total shock: Rohit had gone to Pune to try to ship a large amount of hashish to Europe, but he had been caught, arrested, and imprisoned. I couldn't believe it. What was happening? My poor lover/friend/husband, sitting in an Indian jail? How awful! And what was I to do now? For the second time in a year, I watched my life turn to dust on the floor. I was numb with shock and disbelief.

Busted and Broken

Immediately, I traveled to Pune to see if there was anything I could do. I met up with Dave, an Australian friend of Rohit's, and together we tried to navigate the nightmare of the Indian

136

legal system, chaotic at best, impossible at worst. We couldn't do anything to free Rohit, but I managed to visit him in jail. He was being held in the massive Yerawada Central Prison, which I had passed many times on my way from the Rajneesh Ashram to Pune Airport. It was a huge, high security jail, housing more than 5,000 prisoners. In the old days, during the British Raj, well-known nationalist fighters such as Mahatma Gandhi and Jawaharlal Nehru had been imprisoned there, giving it a certain romantic history. But now it was packed with criminals, people awaiting trial, penniless victims of circumstance, and a scattering of foreigners on drug charges. It was overcrowded, with the stench of stale urine, fear, and desperation filling the air.

When they brought Rohit to meet me, I burst into tears. He looked dirty and bedraggled, and in shock at what had happened to him.

"Oh, my love, my poor, poor love! How can this be happening?" I cried.

"I know," he said, "It's unbelievable. I had no idea when I left you that it would end like this." He sobbed. "I didn't know what I was doing. I thought I could earn some quick money to help us out. But it all went wrong."

We looked at each other in horror and disbelief. This was about as bad as it could be. I knew there was nothing I could do for him. Who knew whether we would ever each other again? All our plans and dreams were shattered. I felt so helpless.

At least, Rohit had access to Westerners who knew how to get aid to him from outside, and his brother was a lawyer in Australia, who pulled as many diplomatic strings as he could. I prayed they could get him out. But it would be a long time before they could navigate the corrupt legal system so that could happen.

Meanwhile, outside, in a state of so-called liberty, I found myself alone once again.

Dark Night of the Soul

Back in London, in my father's flat, I could hear the people passing by on the street outside, the sounds of the London traffic, and the endless rain pouring down. It mirrored my feeling of being in a dungeon of despair. I tossed and turned, my thoughts drifting from the image of Rohit rotting in an Indian jail to memories of my love story with Kumar. I couldn't believe he had simply vanished off the radar; just disappeared, and I could not contact him. Years later, I learned he had returned to Thailand, where he had family, and had become a Buddhist monk.

There was nowhere for me to turn and no escape from these dreadful feelings. A deep, dark depression pulled me into its murky depths. The anxiety and hopelessness I felt when I realized my life was not going forward in the way I had hoped, was too much to bear. I went to bed and pulled the covers over my head. This was the first time I experienced real depression. I could not run, I could not fight, I just had to stop and feel it. All of it. In this bottomless pit, I really felt like I wanted to kill myself. I wanted the ground to open up and swallow me. In that state of helplessness, it felt like my life had come to an end. I truly felt that life was not worth living.

This sinking feeling in my belly was somehow old and familiar; a feeling I had spent my life running from, trying to avoid. I didn't want to feel this way, I'd do anything not to be feeling this hopelessness. I wished I could find some drug to numb myself or drown my sorrows in a bucket of alcohol.

I was in the "nigredo" state, the dark night of the soul, and I was being brought to my knees, and any attempt to manage my life was out of the question. Everything I had done up to this moment was no longer working. The only thing I could do was to stop and feel the pain from which I had been trying to escape. It was the most excruciating time. There was nothing to do, nowhere to go, and no one who could save me. I was in the depths, where I had no choice but to stop, review my life, and in this way unknowingly open the door to my soul's destiny.

138

Chapter Twenty-Seven
A Voice in the Dark

It was 3:00 a.m. and another sleepless night for me. My aching heart and exhausted mind longed for oblivion. I was enduring endless days and countless nights of bleakness. It seemed like a never-ending voyage in darkness.

But then, out of the darkness, I heard a strange voice coming to me. I don't know who or what it was, but it was not my own. It got my attention. It was a woman's voice; maybe it was my mother's voice, or maybe that of a guardian angel I didn't know I had.

It said, "Good."

Good?

"No, it's not good at all. It's very, very bad," I groaned.

"Now we can begin," said the voice, not bothering to respond to my complaint.

It was a loving and kind voice, but at the same time strong and clear.

"Who are you and what are you talking about?" I moaned. "This is not good at all. This is very, very bad."

The voice said, "Never mind. It's time to begin leading your own groups."

I shot up into a sitting position in my bed, astonished at these words.

"What on Earth are you talking about?" I retorted angrily. I wanted to argue. "You can't be serious. I am a hopeless mess. My life is falling apart. I can't do that!"

"That doesn't matter, I will guide you. These groups are to be called 'Awakening the Goddess.'"

This was so ludicrous to me that I almost laughed out loud.

"Awakening the Goddess? That's a joke. How can I teach women about the Goddess? I'll be laughed out of town!"

The voice fell silent, but it had felt so real and so resounding, I couldn't forget it. I had to heed what it said, as it was so clearly coming from deep within me.

And the voice knew better than I did what was needed.

My Purpose Finds Me

After that, I fell asleep and for the first time in a long time I slept well and deeply.

I awoke with a different feeling in my heart. Something strange was happening. I felt held, and somehow guided. This was different from how I had felt in Osho's community, where I knew I belonged but was still so dependent on Osho and my friends. Now it felt like there was a bigger plan and purpose to my life. One that I didn't understand but that I could trust to carry me forward. It was calling me.

The next morning, I sat at breakfast eating the fruit salad and yogurt my dad had prepared, and I told him what the voice had said. He looked at me with his deep blue eyes and smiled a knowing smile.

"I think that is a very good idea," he said. "It's time for you to own your wisdom and share everything you've been learning. I know you have so much to offer other women."

His encouragement was the wind beneath my wings. He supported me all the way and even gave me contacts of women he knew whom he thought would be interested in freeing the feminine within, even though it meant he might lose their business for his own workshops.

Dad had just put on his first workshop in London, in a large and fancy hotel. He had been participating in personal growth workshops in high-end facilities for years, very different from the steamy group rooms of Pune that I had grown to know and love.

His first workshop had been well organized, and I was so touched and proud of my father, facilitating the process with authority and sensitivity, holding each person in a personal process that helped them heal old childhood wounds through guided regression, and step into their own power.

Magician's Journey

Dad's program was called "Journey to the Magician" and drew on the classic psychological metaphor of the Hero's Journey, in which a man goes forth on an adventure, meets all kinds of challenges, is victorious, and comes back transformed.

The aim of Dad's group was to move individuals from feeling like a victim in life to being the masters and creators of their destiny.

They say we teach best what we most need to learn, and I know my father was sharing his own insights and learnings. He had moved through various challenges and was now creating and celebrating his life and the inner freedom he had found.

I remember him saying, "The world teaches us to Do, so that we can Have, and, finally, so that we can just Be. But that's not how it works. Actually, it's the other way around: Be who you are, so that you can Do what you love, and Have what life is offering you. It's already here!"

He lived by those principles and I saw him truly happy and empowered in his life. I assisted him on his first workshop and remember thinking to myself, "Hmm, I can do this too."

For so many years, I had been participating in transformational groups in Pune. Now, I felt like a full sponge, wanting to wring myself out with all the training and experience I had gained.

I was thirty-three and had never had my own vocation in the world. I had no idea how to go about marketing, enrolling, and leading my own groups. But I felt something guiding me, pushing me from the inside, and giving me encouraging signs on the outside.

Paritosh

A few weeks later, I was with friends at a sannyasin gathering at London's Sufi Center. While there was much reverie and laughter in the main hall, I went to the bathroom and took a moment to be quiet and come back to myself.

Standing in front of the mirror, fixing my face, I stood next to an old friend, Paritosh, and found myself admiring her large almond-shaped brown eyes and her thick chestnut bob.

I couldn't help thinking how beautiful she was, despite the age lines on her face. Impulsively, I felt compelled to share my vision with her.

"I am going to start creating a women's group," I said boldly.

Her eyes lit up with excitement. "That's funny. I've been thinking about doing that too. Shall we join forces?"

I loved the way her eyes sparkled and the way she was always ready with a humorous retort and a hearty laugh, with her dry British sense of humor. Even though she was thirteen years older than me, she had tons of energy, and I knew we would make great partners.

"Yes," I replied. "Let's do it!"

Later that week, we spent three days together in my tiny bedroom, in my father's apartment, and cooked up our group.

Sitting there on the floor, we planned the structure, created our processes, and found evocative music to help women get in touch with their anger and their pain, and express all parts of themselves.

Every process we chose was designed to lead them beyond their social identities as women into a deeper experience of what it really means to live, to feel, to heal, and to say, "Yes!" to the wild and wise sacred feminine within.

It would all culminate in a Rite of Passage that required courage for the women to stand in the center of the circle and be witnessed as they bared their bodies, hearts, and souls in nakedness and vulnerability, discovering the unshakeable and unique beauty of their exquisite feminine spirit.

For the first time in my life, I began to trust in my own intuitive guidance and higher calling.

I knew I was in the right place, doing the right thing.

Through all the pain and sorrow of the past weeks and months, being brought to my knees, letting go of my plans... it had allowed deeper plans to unfold within me.

I was surprised how everything, which had just a few weeks earlier seemed so wrong, could now suddenly turn around and feel so right. This was my first conscious experience of the alchemy inherent in transformation.

When we surrender to the darkness and allow ourselves to be cocooned in the shadow, allowing the disintegration and dissolution, something within is working on us—and is transforming us.

Fumbling towards Freedom / Rajyo Allen

Chapter Twenty-Eight
The Goddess in Every Woman

And so, the day arrived. I found myself standing at the front of the room with Paritosh, amazed that in just a few weeks we had managed to fill the group and that I was about to step into my calling as a facilitator and leader.

I had passed through enough "rites of passage" in my own life and was thrilled to be able to offer women a conscious way to do the same, releasing the burden of the past and stepping into a new experience of themselves.

I was so nervous before our event began that I must have brushed my hair and fixed my face about fifty times before the women walked into the room, afraid that I would be judged, found out to be a fraud, or somehow make a fool of myself.

But something in me trusted, and knew it was not me doing this. Rather, something was doing it through me. So even with the nervousness, I felt a sense of calm and groundedness.

Standing there with Paritosh, both of us dressed in our best clothes, we rehearsed what we would say to the twenty-one women who were there to listen and receive what we had to offer them.

As soon as they sat down, we invited them to close their eyes and take a deep breath. I did the same and something relaxed inside of me. All the fears wafted away. I felt Osho's presence with me and remembered that everyone longs for a sense of liberation from the limitations of the mind and the constrictions of social conformity, no matter how cool they seem on the outside.

We were offering an opportunity for these brave and beautiful women to experience their true essence and have that reflected to them. I could feel the hunger for that experience in every participant.

We guided them through processes that involved getting naked, exposing themselves physically and emotionally, expressing their anger and sadness, and freeing up all the wounded, stuck, and frozen places inside.

This was a rite of passage for me as much as for the women. The three-day process washed us clean.

On the last day of the workshop, the final rite of passage took place. Now that they felt safe enough to let themselves be fully seen, they were invited to come to the center of the circle with their sisters sitting all around them, and express whatever wanted to unfold, trusting the Mystery.

Initiation

The center of the circle was an empty space where they could abandon their inhibitions and open to their full expression in the moment, without performing or putting on a show.

Being witnessed by their sisters, and being authentically themselves was a liberating and life changing experience. I was in awe of the incredible beauty of each woman as she bared her soul and often her body, expressing her rage, her fear, her sadness, her vulnerability, and her passion in a full celebration of herself exactly as she is.

In our eyes, every single woman would become radiant and whole. Seeing these women come out in their full glory was deeply rewarding and inspiring. I bowed down to the goddess in each woman. Not the tidy, well managed appearance of the masculine world, not the make-up and held-in stomach of the modern-day woman, strategizing to be accepted and successful in the world. It was so inspiring to see full-on powerful women embracing all of their messy goddess selves.

Every time I would witness a timid, repressed woman become a raging Goddess, I would say to myself, "Yes! Raw, real, and rocking women standing in their true strength and authenticity can change the world!"

I was surprised to see how the women responded to the work. They fell in love with it, and it spread. We continued to do groups in England and in many European countries: Germany, Italy, France, Switzerland, Spain, and Holland. I even took the work to South Africa, the land of my mother's birth, where women could be so repressed. I felt like I was healing my female lineage.

A Great Partnership, Here and Gone

Paritosh was a great partner; she was grounded and practical in her earthy Taurean nature, and dynamic and outrageous at the same time. She was the one who reached out, wrote letters, and found the centers where we could hold our groups. She loved food, and was a great cook; nothing made her happier than sitting down to a sumptuous meal.

We laughed a lot along the way even though we never made much money. We were happy to be travelling and doing work that we loved. Running a business and making money was not our focus or our strength.

On the Euro train from Paris to London, returning from six months of working in Europe, we counted our cash and found that we had just enough money to buy ourselves a nice dinner! We were quite happy to sit down in my father's home and tuck into fish and chips and a pint of English beer.

One day, Paritosh and I were sitting on a bench in the sunshine outside Parimal, a sannyasin center located in the German countryside, where we often used to stop and rest. Paritosh screwed up her beautiful face, turned to me, sighed and said, "I think I'm done."

After five years of travelling and working around Europe, lugging suitcases, and holding space for other women, I could feel her weariness. Ten years older than me, she was going through the roller coaster of menopause and wanted to slow down and take it easy.

"I don't have the bandwidth to do this anymore," she confided. "I'm ready for a change. I don't know what it is, but I want to be more still, spacious, and quiet."

I could feel her longing to find a gentler and more sustaining lifestyle. As for myself, I felt a wince of sadness and fear inside, but I didn't say anything about it. Instead, I honored her decision.

"I support you, my darling, whatever you need to do for your body and peace of mind. I'll carry on from here."

I was sad to lose my dear partner, my wild sister, but I was also touched by the way she just let go with ease and graciousness.

She just shrugged her shoulders, as Osho would say, and moved on. This was something I needed to remember when my time came to let go of the work I had co-created and loved.

I also felt like a change was needed. I heard from friends in California about a new process called the Miracle of Love in San Diego.

Many of my friends were doing this intense ten-day process and called me to come and participate. There it was, dangling like a carrot before me, another chance to make a grab for total freedom, enlightenment, my true self, or whatever it was that I thought was still missing on my spiritual quest. I had to go.

Chapter Twenty-Nine
Miracle of Love

After five years in Europe, I returned to America on New Year's Eve, 1998. I was thirty-nine years old and had no clue as to what my future might hold.

I arrived in San Francisco and flew down to San Diego to a big party to meet my friends. I had no idea what I'd landed in. What the hell was going on here? What was I doing here?

This was the Miracle of Love? It felt more like a bizarre sex party to me. The women were wearing thick makeup, and had long painted nails, fancy clothes, and high heeled shoes.

The men were dancing around a woman called Kalindi, supposedly the guru of this strange phenomena. She had wild curly brunette hair, thick lipstick and a tight look on her face and she was wearing cowboy chaps over a bare butt. She was dancing wildly on the stage. I took an immediate dislike to her; the way she presented herself was an affront to my sense of aesthetics.

This was so different to Osho's sannyas world, where people were naturally beautiful, their inner light shining bright, with a softness and heartfulness to their demeanor.

As an old hippie, I felt out of place here, and my immediate impulse was to run. But something in me made me stay and I decided to jump into the intensive and see what everyone was raving about. This New Year's Eve event kicked off a ten-day process that involved about a hundred participants and at least as many staff members. We were divided in groups of about fifteen and told to sit on chairs arranged in a horseshoe.

There must have been five or six of these horseshoes in the room. Each horseshoe had two facilitators, while the rest of the staff sat at the back of the room, silently observing us.

We were invited to stand up, one by one, and share all the shameful hidden, painful, and uncomfortable stuff that we held inside. Even though I was used to exposing myself in groups and didn't think I had too much left to process, it was terrifying to feel so exposed in front of all these poker-faced strangers.

But as the process got going and I saw my fellow participants standing up and speaking about their experiences, I felt compassion for them, seeing how much we all hold inside that we think is shameful and unacceptable. This created a level of intimacy that I did not expect.

A Battle Within

But intimacy didn't help me every time I went to stand up; I still felt frozen in fear, terrified that how I was presenting was somehow not okay.

I felt my old wound of not being worthy, not good enough to fit in, and found it hard to voice these vulnerable feelings. That started a battle within. The harsh voice of my inner critic told me I should be strong and brave and get up there and do it. The vulnerable part, the traumatized child inside, was unable to do this, requiring gentleness and understanding, not more pressure and judgment.

This inner split, I later understood, reflected a growing division in the late '90s between powerful cathartic therapies and a new, more gentle approach to trauma healing, encapsulated by Peter Levine in his seminal work "Waking the Tiger" and the Somatic Experiencing work he created. Personally, I never considered this to be a question of "either/or." It was more a question of embracing both. Later I trained in Peter Levine's approach and became a somatic therapist, which I found beneficial for healing trauma, both in myself and my clients.

Clearly, the intense pressure generated by the structure in Miracle of Love had nothing to do with a trauma-informed approach. It was intense and it was demanding and encouraged us to go beyond our limits in many ways.

Gradually, for me, there came a time in the horseshoe when the shame and shock subsided and a feeling of blessed relief would arise. It allowed me to connect my inner feelings to my outer expression and then I could see, shining in my fellow participants' eyes, that they really did love and accept me. That was a liberation.

The Burn

After hours of processing in our horseshoes, we were invited to get down on the floor and go through a "Burn Meditation," an intense emotional release session that was accompanied by loud, evocative music. We had a towel in which to scream and a tissue box for the tears.

The only instruction was to allow ourselves to express our emotions fully and let go completely, beating pillows, shouting, weeping, writhing on the floor, dancing... whatever.

Kalindi's message was that the only obstacles standing in the way of union with the divine lay on our side, and the only solution was "unconditional surrender to God!"

For hours, we would burn through the various layers of our ego that were separating us from God and Spirit until we broke open inside, exhausting the mind and opening the heart, so that in the end there was nothing left but the truth of the present moment.

I was more than a little traumatized by the intensity of the experience. Like I said, there was no understanding at that time of the need for sensitivity around trauma healing that we have today. It was a "one-size-fits-all, get-out-of-your-comfort-zone" kind of experience.

Nevertheless, I repeated the process four more times over the next four years, because there was something freeing in being able to expose myself fully, to feel there was nothing to hide.

This helped me understand something Osho had once said: that therapy is an unburdening process which creates a feeling of relief, but it is only temporary.

Unless therapy leads to meditation, it will have to be repeated and again, like cleaning a house that is always accumulating dust.

Staffing the Process

As well as participating, I volunteered to join the staff. Watching others go through the process helped me to be more appreciative of its depth and beauty. Naturally, it was much less scary to sit at the back of the room and watch other people go through it.

My heart ached with empathy and compassion, knowing how it felt for the participants. I fell in love with each person, no matter what their history, and I felt the pain of the human condition that we all experience.

The last time I participated in the Intensive, as it was aptly named, my darling father came and did it with me. Ever the seeker, he, too, longed to unwind his personality structure and uncover his own true identity. Seeing him in his late sixties— when he could have been sitting at home watching TV— standing up in front of the group, exposing his vulnerability, speaking about his wounds, his fears, and his longing, touched me deeply. It made me proud to have such a spiritual warrior for a father.

Am I in the Right Place?

However, as the Miracle of Love expanded it began to feel increasingly like a cult. I had always felt that Kalindi was crazy, but many people saw her as an embodiment of the Indian Goddess Kali, slayer of the ego, and accepted her guidance to get up at 3:00 am and take cold showers, to break up a relationship or find a new partner, and all kinds of other crazy "devices."

I couldn't help comparing Kalindi's erratic behavior with the sensitivity and refinement of Osho, and I was delighted when a group of sannyasin therapists adapted the process, renamed it the Path of Love, and began offering it at the Pune ashram and at other Osho centers.

Meanwhile, back in California, I had found a room in a communal house with other sannyasins. The mama of the house was a cute young German woman whom I remembered from Pune as Bodhitaru, but who now called herself Britta. She lived there with her man and two young boys, along with five other people.

As I had arrived in the USA with no money, I urgently needed a job and soon found myself cleaning houses, a humbling experience after leading my own groups in Europe.

I had fallen sick during my last Miracle of Love session and had developed severe bronchitis, even losing my sense of smell.

I should have been in bed, but I kept pushing myself to get up and go to work, as I needed money to pay my rent and live in California.

I was also battling hopelessness and despair, wondering why I had given everything up in Europe to come here to this insane program.

I wanted to get away, but there was nowhere to go. I just had to face the situation, accepting that I had no idea how things were going to change.

Chapter Thirty
Celebration of Being

One evening after dinner, when the kids were asleep, Britta and I sat drinking beer in the messy kitchen, determined to leave the washing up for someone else.

"Tell me about your work in Europe" she said to me

"Well, it was about giving women permission to be all that they can be," I said, hesitantly, a little embarrassed because I did not feel like a good example of what I was sharing."

I added, "We help women to remember who they truly are when freed from the shackles of society's conditioning. It's about freeing the 'Sacred Feminine' in women."

As I talked about the work, I could feel my tired body becoming energized and the fire in my heart being rekindled. Britta looked at me with her soft brown eyes and said:

"You have to do that here! It sounds amazing, and I want to experience it."

It was the spark I needed. Slowly, slowly, talking to friends, asking around, I managed to organize a group and a few months later we were sitting with a group of women in a rustic community building in Muir Beach, just outside Mill Valley.

The waves crashed on the rocks below and expansive skies reached out towards an oceanic horizon. It was the perfect place to hold my first event. I had no staff and most of the participants were my peers who, despite a tendency to be rebellious, all showed up for the program.

On the final afternoon, during the initiation ceremony, I could see Britta was in awe of the women in the center.

Her eyes were shining with tears of recognition and appreciation, seeing each woman's essence.

I don't know how I managed to run that group on my own, but something came through and everyone had a transformative experience.

A New Partner

At the end of the group, as I sat on the outside deck and breathed in the success of holding my first event, single-handedly in America, Britta approached me and knelt beside me very excited.

"You have to do this work. It is so important!"

Her recognition gave me the courage and strength to begin my work in America.

Britta had been leading a singing workshop called "Breakthrough Performance," but as soon as she could, she extricated herself in order to join me as an equal partner. Before long, we started leading women's groups, adding more form and structure to the process.

I had no manual and tended to lead groups from my own intuition, trusting the spontaneity of the moment.

But Britta, being the practical German that she is, really grounded the work and its format. With her passion for Truth and her lover's heart, she gave everything to bringing the workshops forth and I was grateful for her partnership.

As a result, in the year 1999, the process formerly known as "Awakening the Goddess" was reborn in California as "Celebration of Woman." From there we created the umbrella organization "Celebration of Being."

It wasn't long before we began to consider the men. Why can't we bring this profound work, which has been so liberating for women, to our male counterparts? Our friend Michael, who was a facilitator himself, shook his head at the idea.

"You are crazy, how can women possibly lead a group for men? You know nothing about men's issues!"

He had a point but was also missing the point.

"It's true, we don't know men's issues specifically," I told him. "But we do know about love. We know that everybody needs love, and everybody has old hurts and wounds that cause them to protect and defend their hearts. We know how to help them heal and open their hearts to love again."

The Noble Man

Michael's doubts were a provocation, galvanizing our belief that we did indeed have something to offer men, and so the "Celebration of the Noble Man" was born, entirely led and staffed by women.

It was revolutionary, it was radical, and it worked. The men came, and whatever their issues were with women got mirrored back to them. The women were willing to play the roles of their mothers, their wives, or their schoolteachers, or whoever had castrated and disempowered them.

The men also had an opportunity to open to the divine feminine and see how they could come into "right relationship" with women, without projecting a mother figure onto them, or expecting women to be a certain way.

They could experience the true masculine in themselves and the true feminine in women, and the alchemical transformation that was tangible.

The first time we held the initiation ceremony, we were nervous. Men don't just "let go" like women do. They are more in their heads, planning and strategizing their way through life.

But there is an alchemical force moving through each one of us, the pull of true nature, the call of spirit, the whispering of our hearts that longs to be felt and to be free.

We were not disappointed. We witnessed the true masculine being expressed through these men, as their tender, raw, and courageous essences came through.

The beauty of a man standing in his true power, showing up as the warrior and protector of women and all that is fragile in life was visible for all to see.

The Noble Man process changed men's lives, as it changed their relationships with women. I boldly declared that we were healing the world, one heart at a time, knowing that healing is possible when men and women are willing to be vulnerable and share their wounds.

The Power of Love

It was remarkable for men to have an opportunity to step out of being either emasculated and collapsed, or defensive and macho, and to come into an open-hearted relationship with themselves and the women around them. Real men and real women were coming together at last.

The next step was to reverse the roles. Britta and I sat down in her house and cooked up a series of beautiful processes to help women heal their pain in the presence of the men. The Power of Love workshop was born.

As you can imagine, it required courage for women to allow themselves to be vulnerable in this way, as they have experienced so much abuse, abandonment, and betrayal from men. But, once again, incredible healing was experienced as the women began to trust that men could be present and meet them and hold them with vulnerability and love.

Within a short time, all the workshops we were running —as many as one a month for years—kept us busy.

During the four days that each workshop lasted, we would be working from 6:00 a.m. until midnight. At last, I felt I was truly living my purpose.

I was able to channel something larger than myself that needed to be transmitted to the world.

With every man or woman going through the initiation process, I would affirm aloud, "This is one more heart we are healing, and the world is a little more loving, kind, and peaceful because of it."

Sitting in that circle, witnessing men and women break down and sob as they released years of pain, touched something in me that was also broken, yet also beautiful.

I could see my own wounds and embrace them more fully. I could feel the beauty in my own journey.

I saw it, too, in the eyes of the men and women going through the program. "Here I am, see me, feel me, I am finally free!" And all the brothers and sisters sitting in the circle would be shedding tears of recognition, with smiles of unconditional love, and silently affirming "Yes you are!"

It was not long before we created leadership trainings to allow others to learn to offer this work. I loved the training, because it allowed me to be engaged and intimate with people as they learned the skills and tools needed to become leaders in their own right.

It was fulfilling work and the community around us grew.

Participants would come back as staff members and then join us in the training to learn to facilitate the work.

"Unwrap your Presence" was an eight-day training we offered, and over time it evolved into a three-part, year-long opportunity to acquire group-leading skills in a more general way.

Over time, we birthed many brilliant facilitators to lead this deep, embodied, heart-centered work.

Chapter Thirty-One
Cancer Meditation

I lay there frozen on the table and watched in horror as the doctor stuck a long cold surgical needle into several places in my breast, including straight into my nipple.

The pain seared through my body like a hot iron. I left her office howling like a wild animal with a bullet wound. The prescribed painkillers did nothing to ease my agony. What was growing in my breast was a 9.5-centimeter tumor that was silently stalking me, and it had my number.

I felt sick to my stomach. *"This is my death sentence,"* I thought. All I could do was try to stay in the present moment, as thinking about what might happen was just too scary. I had to keep my feet on the ground, my attention in the Now. But my fear was palpable, visceral, unrelenting. It was the fear of the child who lost her mom and doesn't know what's going to happen to her. Where would I be without my physical health?

The wise ones of Tibet say that to be born into a human body is as rare as a blind turtle in an infinite ocean finding its way to the surface in order to pop its head up through a rubber ring.

That is how precious it is to have a body, to experience life and the possibility of waking into Consciousness. This body is a temple of the Spirit; a rare blessing of infinite Grace that gives us the opportunity to work through our karma and attain liberation. One sunny day in California, back in 2000, life was offering me just that.

Of course, I should have known. The lump in my breast had been growing steadily. After many months of working with my thermographer she had, at last, been forced to admit that it was more than an ordinary lumpy breast and that I really should go for a second opinion. I had put off doing that for a while, not wishing to hear the dreaded "C" word.

Back home in England, the free National Health Service would have covered me, but in America, without health insurance, I envisioned myself homeless and alone with this disease ravaging my body. In spite of a strong fear of doctors and western medicine, which I sawd as "white-coat phobia," I made it to the doctor's office accompanied by my boyfriend, Ray, and Britta. Gripping their hands to help me cross the threshold, I hoped and prayed this medical expert would find nothing.

Finding Out

The doctor, her attitude as crisp as her white coat, addressed me without emotion. I remember wondering how she could be so cool when she had my life in her hands. I felt dirty and disgusting, the mark of death upon me. She smeared cool sticky gel over my inflamed breast and rolled the sonogram sensor over the area. I waited for her to say something, but she was silent about the large lump in my left breast. I breathed a sigh of relief when she said, "I don't see anything abnormal here."

I was about to get up and go, but something in me pulled me back. I could have settled for the answer she gave, but I was not convinced."I need to know," I blurted out. "What else can you do? Aren't there other ways of testing?"

"We can do a biopsy," she said in a detached manner, then left and returned a few minutes later with a fine needle. I squirmed at the thought of that cold, sharp needle going into my tender bosom. The reality was far worse than I had imagined.

Three endless days later, I got the call to go to the doctor's office, and a sickening dread filled me. My legs were so weak they could barely carry me. I shivered with chills even though the summer sun baked my skin. Armed once again with my support team—Ray and Britta—I entered the doctor's office.

She pronounced the words I dreaded hearing: "You have ductal carcinoma in situ. It needs to be dealt with quickly; it's already grown to very large proportions."

"What do I need to do?" I asked, not wanting the answer.

"You'll need to have intensive chemotherapy to try to shrink the mass. Then they will need to operate and hope they get clear margins. We won't know if they can save your breast, or if they will need to perform a full mastectomy." The doctor looked at me with a mixture of compassion and brisk efficiency.

Tough Choices

I stood somewhere outside my body watching this whole interaction. The only thing holding me in place was the intense pain lingering in my breast from the needle, a reminder that I was about to go on an excruciating journey, which I was not sure I had the strength to complete. If I did not die of the cancer, then surely the chemotherapy and other aggressive treatments would kill me.

The next days, weeks, and months were marked by intensive research into all western and alternative methods of treatment. I needed to find a way to treat this disease that was kind to my body and my frayed nervous system. I began to explore holistic options, agonizing over each decision, knowing the life I had thus far taken for granted could soon be over. I had to trust the way would be shown to me.

I went to several oncologists and was not happy with their responses. The first oncologist was an older man with smooth grey hair on a head that had seen many cases—I was just the next one in a long line. Without any bedside manner that respected me, my life, and my feelings, he said:

"You will need to do chemotherapy immediately. We need to treat this aggressively, otherwise you will be dead within a year." He looked piercingly at me after writing his notes. I was shaking but I held his gaze. How could he say that with such certainty? Some willful streak arose in me, and I vowed to prove him wrong. I walked out of his office and swore I would never have him as my doctor.

On My Own

Now I was on my own, but a new resolve was arising in me: to find my way before the cancer took over my whole body. It was such a strange feeling, to not be at home in my own body. This once trusted friend had now become a betrayer that could abandon me at any moment. I began to ask deeper questions, "Who am I really? If this body is what I have taken myself to be, who will I be without it? Will I still "Be" without it?"

Cancer is a unique journey for each person. Everyone must find their own way with what feels right. It is a journey not only of curing cancer, but of healing the body, mind, and soul. Some people make it, some don't, no matter what method they choose. Until you're faced with such a life-threatening disease, it's impossible to know how it'll impact you.

I opted for the alternative method and went all out to try to heal myself. I wanted to understand what had caused my cells to turn cancerous, so I began intense therapy. What were the physiological, emotional, and spiritual causes of my illness? Had it begun long ago in childhood, with the early shock of losing my mother? Or was it the constant stress and anxiety I'd been living with these past ten years? Was it the volatile and unstable relationship I found myself in with Ray? Was it my recent abortion that had disrupted my hormones? Or was it the soul's journey, at a crossroads, pointing me in another direction, giving me no choice but to listen to the whispering— now screaming—cry of my inner being? I left no stone unturned in my psyche to get to the roots.

I did everything I could to heal my body. I spent a fortune on supplements, and positively rattled from all the vitamins I was taking. These changed every week as my naturopath determined what needed detoxing and what needed tonifying inside. I changed my diet to raw meat, eggs, cream, milk, and vegetable juice, as advised by one member of my health care team who'd analyzed my blood. I managed to add 30 pounds to the 100 pounds I had weighed when I had been diagnosed. No one believed I was sick, I looked so plump and healthy.

Chapter Thirty-Two
I'm not ready to Die

I travelled to Brazil to see Joao de Deus (John of God), the psychic healer, who performed miraculous surgeries on people with his bare hands. I'd heard of his mysterious healing power and was hopeful he could remove the cancer in my breast.

When I arrived there, I saw people who had been disabled get up and walk. There was a room full of discarded crutches and wheelchairs. Every day, I would walk from the inn, where I stayed, to the Casa where John of God presided. Everyone was dressed in white and looked pure and angelic.

After drinking fresh coconut water for breakfast, we would line up and wait to be seen by John of God. He would look at me for a few seconds and either prescribe surgery, in which case I would go into the "surgery room" and wait until he came, or I would go to the healing room with many others, singing prayers and receiving the healing energy.

When receiving a "surgery" I'd lie on a bed in a large room with other patients. John of God would work on most patients with a rusty knife, inserting it into a certain part of their bodies, but with me, he would use scissors, sticking them way up a nostril, farther than one could do physically and still expect survival. I received this kind of surgery on three different occasions. There was never any pain and no blood, even though there was no anesthesia.

After a "surgery," patients were told to go back to the guest house to rest for twenty-four hours. As I lay on my bed, all kinds of visions came to me, and I often found myself shaking, trembling with fever, undergoing strong emotional release, and then I would experience a sense of relaxation and deep peace. Sometimes I slept for twenty-four hours, as my body underwent this healing process.

Four long years passed while I did everything I could possibly think of, and I spent many thousands of dollars, which miraculously kept coming to me through fundraisers and the generous support of my beloved community, far and wide. Yet still my life was hanging in the balance between life and death.

I could feel death stalking me, and I felt my will to live slipping away. I'd lay in bed at night and think of my loved ones, my friends and family, my two-year-old goddaughter, Sierra, and how we'd feel if we couldn't see each other anymore. I thought of my darling brother, who has struggled with such pain from his condition all his life, who made a vow at fourteen never to complain, to not be a victim in life. He has gone on to become such a force of good in the world, speaking out against social injustice with his creativity, creating a whole genre with his music, travelling all over with his group, Test Dept. I've always been inspired by the power that comes through him to overcome his pain with his passion. Where was my passion? I had to find it within me somehow.

Radical and Fast

Finally, I awoke early one morning and took a long hard look at myself in the bathroom mirror. My tumor had not shrunk, in fact it had now taken over the whole of my left breast. It was the size of a grapefruit. There was also a golf ball-sized tumor under my left armpit. It was spreading to my lymph system. I needed to do something radical, and fast. It was now clear that I needed to find a western doctor to help me. I had to put aside my mistrust of western medicine and change course if I was to live to tell the tale. If I didn't to do this, I was going to die.

I went to see my next-door neighbor, Mark, who had just been diagnosed with liver cancer, and asked him how his treatment was going. "Do you like your oncologist?" I asked eagerly.

"He's a great guy," said Mark. "He's really available and very heartful." I noticed I took a deep breath. Life was showing me my next step. That meeting with my neighbor guided me to meet the man who'd be the main help in my healing process.

The next day, I was sitting in the office of Dr. Ari Baron, whose gentle demeanor and kind brown eyes soothed my nervousness and made me feel cared for. He sat and listened intently as I told him the whole story of my cancer journey. It was as if he had nowhere else to go and nothing he'd rather do than listen to me. I know he had a ward full of cancer patients waiting to see him but, in his presence, I felt like the most important person in the world. After a few moments reviewing my file, he turned towards me. "We're going to go for full recovery," he said simply, and smiled in a way that melted my fear, like ice in the warm sun. I almost jumped out of my skin! I had expected him to say, "We'll do what we can," or "I am sorry, it's too late."

Chemo

In that moment I breathed a deep sigh of relief. I felt I could lay my life in this man's hands and together we would make it. That was four-and-a-half-years after I had been diagnosed and I had already outlived the first oncologist's prognosis for me.

In January 2005, I walked into the University of California San Francisco (UCSF) hospital for my first round of chemo. I saw the people lying there, receiving the drug they hoped would save their lives. I prayed it would save mine. I was forty-four years old. I still had a lot of life in me. I lay down and let the nurses stick the needle into my veins to have the toxic chemical concoction pumped throughout my system. It was a relief to stop worrying whether I was doing the right thing. I was doing the only thing left.

The next four months were spent in regular rounds of chemo, going in every two weeks for the treatment, spending several days feeling like crap, then doing a series of acupuncture and alternative treatments to help me recover and prepare for the next round. If I had not spent the previous four years building up my health and putting on weight, I feel sure the chemo would have ravaged me. But it was not as bad as anticipated. Every time they pumped the poison into my veins, I told myself this was good medicine. When I saw the tumor shrinking after the first few treatments, I knew that it really was.

167

Saving My Life

The pharmaceutical companies I had so hated and feared were now saving my life. I let go of my angry stories about corporations exploiting people for profit and surrendered to the wonders of modern science. Weeks turned into months and as the tumor disappeared, so did my hair. It began to fall out in clumps, and I looked like a mangy orphan. My girlfriend finally came over and cut off all my locks. She donated the hair to "Wigs for Children" who were going through chemo. As for myself, I wasn't into wearing a wig. I enjoyed having no hair to wash, dry, or style. It was just me in my nakedness. I felt bold and beautiful, even though the chemo was a rough ride. At the end of four months, I was amazed that the tumor had shrunk to nothing, and my breast appeared to be normal again. I was over the moon with joy.

But the work was far from over. Next came the surgery. My wonderful oncologist had a good team of fellow doctors and we decided to begin with a lumpectomy, not a full-blown mastectomy. But, alas, they did not get good margins and could not guarantee all cancerous cells had been removed. By that time, I was so tired I just said, "Do whatever you need to do to save my life. If you have to take off my breast, go ahead."

I remember being asked if I wanted to go for a reconstruction, but when I thought of the implications, the further surgeries, transplanting fat (which I did not have) and muscle from other parts of my body, I said, "No, just take off my breast; I'm tired of my body being messed about."

Normally I am a vain creature, but at this point I had no doubt it was better to live to tell the tale than to look good on my deathbed. Off to surgery I went. I remember the anesthetic going into my veins and then I was out cold, gone to a dreamy world where all was well.

Vaguely, as I drifted away, I remembered why I loved narcotics: the feeling of being far beyond the cares of this world is a blessed relief.

Chapter Thirty-Three
Imperfect Body

The next thing I knew was waking up without my left breast. Heavily bandaged, my chest was flat and raw.

When the anesthetic wore off it felt sore, with a tube draining the fluids away. I was woozy from the anesthetic and numb as to what this meant for me as a woman. I was glad to be alive, that much I knew, and I was one step closer to being free from cancer.

It was several months before I healed; a bad staph infection slowed down the healing, and I had to take several courses of antibiotics. After this there was several months of radiation that I endured before I was through the treatments. 2005 was my year of radical treatments to save my life.

Now I had to get used to living minus one breast. I was healed from the operation and now had to heal as a woman. My family had always been naked with each other, and I'd always felt comfortable being naked around other people. But now I found myself being more cautious about who was going to see my scarred and naked form, as they might wince or recoil. This was my lesson now: to love my perfectly imperfect body.

I no longer had a Barbie doll figure. My shape was ravaged and ruined but I was grateful to be alive. I heard that the women of the Amazon tribe of female warriors would cut off their breasts deliberately in order to be better archers and hunters, and I was learning to accept the warrior in me: older and wiser, with the scars to show that I had been to battle.

They say that after five years cancer is in remission, but it's only ten to fifteen years later that you can actually say, "I'm fully on the other side of it."

After the cancer operation, I vowed to live each day as totally as possible, and came to understand what Osho always said, "The people who are most afraid of death are the ones who have not fully lived."

Goodbye to Ray

Another realization dawned on me. Going through menopause, surviving breast cancer, I knew it was time to end my relationship with Ray. Things had never been easy between us. We had loved each other intensely, and he had done his best to be supportive during my difficult cancer journey, but there was always a storm brewing between us that could erupt at any moment.

Ray was a beautiful man with a deep soul, a photographer and poet, but he could also be very emotional and reactive. Even though we laughed and played together, and he held me tenderly in my most terrified moments, our fights were intense and explosive, erupting over the tiniest things on which we could not agree. Somehow our combined chemistry proved highly combustible and, in both of us, fury and frustration could reach the boiling point in seconds.

After the chemo and surgery, I knew that what my body and nervous system needed more than anything else was rest and quiet. Ray knew it, too, and sorrowfully we understood the situation and let each other go. I took myself off to a cottage in the countryside where I could be alone, in retreat from the world, and walk the hills of West Marin.

I was entering a period of isolation, moving out on my own and spending a great deal of time in Nature, integrating all I had gone through.

Alone in my little rented cottage, I often sat and stared at the walls, which reflected back to me the emptiness I felt inside. I felt no impulse to go anywhere or do anything. I just had to sit and face myself and let the emptiness be there, until something else wanted to happen.

170

I didn't know it at the time, but I was undergoing an alchemical process, waiting in the blackness, in the dark and empty void, until the time when something new was meant to happen.

I had been in this place before but now had no energy to resist. Even when friends were around me, I was adrift inside myself. I didn't try to fill the hole. I just had to be with it. So much had been stripped away, so much had gone. Who was I now? I had been humbled, I was less arrogant, less smart, less aggressive, somehow softer, more tender, and hopefully wiser.

It took me several years to learn how to be in relationship with myself again and become comfortable with my aloneness. I had encountered death. In a sense, I had been reborn. Much of my self-image had gone, along with my dreams of relationship and family, plus the romantic notion that there is a permanent state called "happily ever after."

In a way, I had come to know, up close and personally, that there is no such thing as a perfect life. It is messy, it is painful, it is ugly, and it is uncomfortable in all its raw beauty and fleeting fragility.

Phoenix from the Ashes

Slowly, out of these insights, arose acceptance and peace. Sitting in my garden, relishing my aloneness, happy with the company of my beautiful blue-eyed Burmese Himalayan cat, Princess, I realized I had found, for the first time in my life, a deeper contentment. It took five years for me to integrate this.

And then... well, isn't that just like Life? As soon as I'd found my authentic aloneness, back came the promise of togetherness, knocking on my door. I'll be darned if that wasn't when the man who would become my future husband stepped in.

Vinit had had his eyes on me for more than twenty years—since the ashram days in India. We had bumped into each other a few times in Marin and had shared a breath work training together.

Most of that time we had both been in relationships with other people. Finally, the time was right, and we were available.

I was not looking for a relationship at that time—so content in my aloneness was I—but he reached out to me, saying he'd like to get together for a walk. I think it took a year for me to agree to that walk, as I was hesitant and cautious, but he was persistent. I felt shy of relationships and not at all sure of myself as a woman. But he wooed me ever so gently.

We walked through the flower-filled meadow outside his home and enjoyed each other's company. It was nice to feel a man's interest in me as a woman again.

A short while later he came around for tea, and we chatted and warmed to each other some more. He left his shoes outside my door. For a month.

I kept wondering why he didn't come to pick his shoes up. Maybe this was his way of saying he was moving in. I was not sure I wanted that. Today I know he goes barefoot whenever he can and leaves his shoes all over the place. It wasn't a romantic gesture on his part. But, for sure, he managed to keep his foot in my door!

Chapter Thirty-Four
True Love

Eventually, Vinit wrote me an e-mail inviting me on a date.

"We will both keep our clothes on, and just hold each other. We don't have to kiss or get sexual."

I was surprised and curious. And touched by his respect. I hadn't been with a man for five years and I wasn't sure I could ever be sexual again, so I let him know he would need to go slowly. He was fine with that. After all, he had been married to—and well trained by—an experienced Tantra teacher and knew how to go at the woman's pace.

I was enticed by his invitation and said, "Yes."

We held each other, we kissed, and we found we had chemistry together. The first time I showed him my naked body, I said, "Maybe you are not going to love all of me."

"On the contrary" he said, "I already love all of you." He looked at my naked body admiringly. And he did love all of me. My missing breast was not an issue. And he adored my slender frame, whereas some men have thought me too skinny and not womanly enough.

Vinit loved the sinewy structure of my form, and the way our lithe bodies fitted together. I knew he was interested in me, not just my body. Somehow our souls had been waiting for the right moment to find each other. He told me he loved me and had been waiting a long time for me. He helped me soften and open once more to my feminine self. Gradually, I could feel my sharp edges—that had been braced against the world for so long—begin to soften and melt.

173

Even though I knew I could be difficult and demanding, at times petulant, emotional, and unpredictable, I also discovered a trust that Vinit's love for me was rock solid.

A Perfect Match

For the longest time in our relationship, and even after we married, we did our own thing, meeting briefly and beautifully but spending many days and even weeks apart, living in two homes, one in town and the other in the countryside.

For the first several years, we had a strange relationship. Both lovers of freedom and with different areas of focus, we enjoyed living our lives in our own chosen ways. It was an ongoing journey of growing intimacy and commitment that eventually led to us getting married with a wonderful wedding celebration.

Our two worlds came together: him handing me a skydiving suit so I could experience the heights with him; me handing him a deep-sea diving suit so he could plumb the depths with me.

Even though we are very different, we complement each other well. Our biggest love and greatest passion is creating beauty and sacredness in our lovely home and retreat center in Asheville, North Carolina. In workshops, we make a good team: he offers the worldly focus, bringing awareness to issues like climate change and social justice. I guide people into meditation and to become more present and awake as human beings.

The Gift of Life

Before cancer, I didn't appreciate how dear this body and this life are to me. My journey has been one of extremes; the years of drugs, self-abuse, and illness have taken their toll. These days, my body is not as strong as it used to be. My spirit continues to race ahead tirelessly, but my body often wants to slow down, taking more time to smell the roses in the garden, appreciating the simpler things of life, such as the profound miracle of waking up each day and experiencing a deep breath moving through my lungs, my heart beating, and the sunshine and blue sky seen through the bedroom window.

I am both tremendously resilient and incredibly fragile. If I had not had cancer, I might not have appreciated the precious gift of life: to have a body, to be able to walk and talk and sing and dance. I love to eat, make love, be silly, and laugh; to look into another's eyes and say, "I love you," and mean it, because we may not get another chance.

Suffering as Grace

The challenges I have experienced are nothing compared to those people who go through long-drawn-out illnesses or sustain near-fatal, life-changing injuries. I consider myself fortunate to have a body that can get up and walk across the room without effort. I am lucky enough to live in a place where I eat healthy food and drink clean water. And I thank God every day that I made it through to tell the tale.

I would never voluntarily choose suffering, but I know that suffering can be embraced as Grace; that those who face extreme physical challenges are often the kindest and most loving people. As we learn the lessons life teaches us, we begin an alchemical process inside ourselves that creates the possibility of "The Divine Human." This is the opportunity on this plane, to transmute dense reality, expressed through the physical body, into an experience and expression of Divine Consciousness.

We are invited to transfigure these bodies to become vessels of Spirit, and messengers of Light, or Grace Delivery Devices, as my teacher Miranda says. This is no easy task, as we flounder through the mire of this dimension. The sickness and disease so many are experiencing is a symptom of a larger sickness affecting us all, the disconnection from our own soul, and from Mother Earth herself.

175

It takes discipline to remember what is truly important in this life and to return to a sense of love, care, and respect for ourselves. Life provides us with many wakeup calls, including cancer. For me, it was a reminder that something wasn't working, and I had to change my ways.

I am still integrating what cancer has taught me. This life is a gift, and it is not for me to take it for granted. It is an incredible privilege to be here, and to be given the opportunity to love and to offer myself in love. Now I understand that it all had to start from within.

Perfectly Imperfect

I should perhaps mention that when Vinit and I got together I was using a prosthetic breast, which was often a hilarious experience. Sometimes I would bend over and...plop! It would fall out of my bra and onto the floor. There were times when I stunned onlookers with my removable breast. It looked okay underneath my clothes and tucked into my bra. But when I took my clothes off, reality emerged and anyone could see the non-breast side of my chest was flat and raw, while the other breast was loose and becoming floppier with age.

It was quite a sight, and I did not feel attractive when I was naked, even though I often showed my bare body in my workshops and at the local hot springs. I never really became proficient at wearing the prosthesis and quite frankly, over time, it was getting to be a drag.

So, I decided that it might be time to get reconstructive surgery and give Vinit and myself the pleasure of two normal breasts.

This began a whole other adventure. The surgeon tried to pump up my irradiated skin, over an extended period, gradually inflating the breast. He inserted an expander, to force the radiated tissue to stretch. I had a synthetic breast implanted, which didn't look real but at least in clothes it appeared to be natural and normal. Without clothes I looked, well, a little lopsided at best.

My darling man always loved and accepted me, bless his noble heart, but my body was no longer what it was. I started to feel self-conscious. I was still leading workshops and when we'd all get naked, I'd be there with my strange-looking boobs, exposing the misshapen body underneath my clothes.

From Implants to Explants

It was a paradoxical situation. On the one hand, I saw myself as an example to women that we could have all kinds of body issues and there was never any need to be ashamed. But, on the other hand, after several reconstructive surgeries and ten years of trying, I realized that the effort to make my breasts look normal simply wasn't working.

Then, on a medicine journey, ingesting the sacred San Pedro cactus, I received clear guidance to have my implants removed. I was also hearing from several girlfriends about the possibility of Breast Implant Illness. Although I didn't feel particularly sick, I was made aware of the toxicity that these foreign objects could create in my body. Yuck.

I found a surgeon in Mexico and booked a flight to Guadalajara. Within weeks, I had reversed years of messing with my boobs in vain attempts to be normal, and my implants became ex-plants.

So here I am now, seventeen years after my cancer journey, a woman with one breast. The place where the other one used to be is scarred and flat. I accept myself this way and I take comfort from that legendary tale of the female Amazon warriors who cut off their breasts to shoot more easily with bow and arrow when they went into battle. I know now to pick my battles more carefully. And I'm happy to say I've already won this one.

Chapter Thirty-Five
Who Am I Really?

Even during the cancer treatment and recovery I had continued leading workshops and trainings, grateful to have a bigger purpose and be able to share my passion for transformation. But now, twenty years after I had started the work in England and fifteen years after Celebration of Being had been birthed in America, I felt tired of running workshops.

I was increasingly dragging myself through these intense processes and I noticed I was less and less excited about the work. Quite honestly, at the age of fifty-five and recovering from cancer, I longed for a rest. I lay in bed one morning and could hear the faint whisper of that inner guidance telling me to "Let go, just let go."

My partner, Britta, was having to carry more of the load and I knew she was becoming resentful. Despite my urging to change the format to make things less intense, we carried on offering intense four-day workshops and longer trainings. One morning, meeting up with her in a coffee shop, I put down my cup and said, "You know, Britta, I think I'm done. I don't think I can carry on much longer."

Britta listened intently and sympathetically. I know she had frequently felt the same way. But I was scared to lose her friendship as well as her partnership, and all that we had created and shared together. We had been through so much together: love and loss, pain and joy, an intense longing for the Truth, and a passion to share healing and transformation with others. We were sisters, and friends, and she had been the comforting presence of a mother figure for me. We called each other husband and wife (interchangeably!), as we were practically married to each other. As partners we had created so many radical healing experiences for others.

But now it was all changing. The next thing I knew we were in mediation with a business coach, a wise and wonderful woman called Mary, who had helped me begin the work in America and had coached us both before; she had agreed to preside over the terms of the breakup.

Britta and her husband Lee sat on one side of the conference table, and I was alone on the other side, feeling that this was all happening way too fast, even though I had triggered the process. I know Britta was ready for change and I felt I was taking up the space that Lee could step into to help her run the business.

Mary looked at me and asked, "What do you want to happen?"

I had no idea what I wanted. I couldn't think. I knew I needed a change, but I didn't know what that would look like. I felt like I had to say something, even though I felt very shaky.

"I… I'm willing to give up the Celebration of Woman, the Noble Man, and the Power of Love," I stammered, feeling like a mother who has spent nine months carrying a baby and was now giving it up for adoption. There was a lump in my throat, and I could hardly speak. My voice seemed to be coming from another planet.

"But I still want to facilitate the Leadership Training," I blurted out, trying desperately to hold onto something.

The Shock of Letting Go

It was all very business-like. Suddenly Britta had another partner. She didn't need me anymore and I was out of the picture. Now she was pulling away. We worked out the logistics and within a few days I was presented with a contract, saying our partnership was over. I signed and from that moment was officially cut off from any involvement in the business, not to mention divorced from our sisterhood and robbed of my connection with the community. Suddenly I had lost my identity in the world, and I had no sense of purpose. I was in a state of shock and disbelief. I had hoped I could be grand-mothered out, and still have some connection to the work. But it wasn't like that. I was suddenly very alone. I experienced an unbearable sense of loss and shame from the broken sense of belonging

My first reaction was to try and find new footing. I spent a lot of money on marketing courses, scrambling to recreate myself and generate a new business venture, called "Alchemy of Awakening," which had been bubbling inside me for a while. Although I was excited about this new direction, I was also desperately trying to re-constellate the sense of self I had known when I was leading workshops with Britta, entirely forgetting that the main reason why I'd quit was because I was exhausted and needed a break.

"If only I can get my business going, everything will be fine," I told myself, trying hard not to feel the grief of knowing that I had lost so much more than my role in the business. I was in a deep state of shock and trauma. This wasn't how I had expected it to happen. I felt alone and bereft, losing not only my partnership, but also my community, my clients and my purpose. And my identity.

My girlfriend Ali kept telling me to slow down and take time to let things settle. Wise words. But in vain. So, Ali and Vinit had to watch me tie myself into a pretzel, resisting their suggestions to chill out. None of my plans were working. Even though I was trying hard and running fast, life had other ideas. My soul required me to be exactly where I was: in no man's land. Eventually it became clear, even to me, that if anything was going to happen, it wouldn't happen through my effort or will. I needed to let go and let existence take care.

I spent many months grieving my losses, wishing I could be back in the groups where my passion for transformation felt so alive, and I knew my place and my purpose. Instead, I had to turn and face the endless emptiness inside. When I finally surrendered, my sense of loss gave way to a feeling of relief. I had to acknowledge the reality: I was tired and burnt out. Just to be able to lie in bed in the morning, let my body rest and not know what the day would bring, was deeply relaxing.

The Need to be Needed

Osho always said that a woman's downfall is her need to be needed. I could see how much I'd been getting my own narcissistic supply of being needed from my clients, my participants, my partnership, and my relationship with the business. Suddenly all of that was gone and I was surprised by the amount of trauma that opened up inside me, touching old wounds of loss, betrayal, and abandonment. I had heard Osho say many times that we don't want to face our aloneness, because when we do, we have to pass through these horrible feelings of isolation and loneliness, and the endless aching wound of our unworthiness.

I was surprised by my shakiness, as I'd always considered myself a good meditator, able to spend long hours with myself in retreat, sitting silently on a cushion. But this was different. There was no peace of mind. Rather, I was driving myself crazy, looking back over my shoulder, reminiscing and ruminating. I felt stuck. I could not go back, and I could not move forward. Yet, even in my most tormented times, there were moments when I simply had to surrender. When I did, I was able to find peace in the present moment, together with a reassuring sense that some mysterious power or force beyond me was always holding and supporting me.

Loss of identity strips us of that which we have taken ourselves to be. We are not who we think we are. As I grappled with the loss of my work, I had to remind myself: "I'm not that person. I'm not my job. I'm not the great facilitator...." Conceptually, I had always known this. It is basic to all spiritual teachings, spelled out to me so many times: you are not your personality, your ego, your social self. But only now that was it being fully brought home to me.

Too Much, Too Fast

As I mentioned earlier, we experience trauma when things happen too much, too fast, too soon. It had happened that way for me as a child, when I lost my mum, and it felt that way now, in giving up my work. Feeling like I had no meaning, and my life had no purpose, was the most painful thing for me. What was my life about if I wasn't serving others or contributing in some way?

Only now can I see that this painful process was a necessary peeling away of layers of false identity. I had to confront my naked, utter emptiness. I didn't know how or when this would end, but I knew on some level that I had to go through it. Inadvertently, I had landed in the place of asking the perennial spiritual question: "Who am I? Really?"

Groping in the dark—facing the void in my life, feeling the hole inside and not being able to fill it—gradually brought me to a point of realization: I don't need to be anybody in particular, or anybody special, in order to know my essence. I have value and self-worth just as I am, right now.

Resting in emptiness proved to be the secret that had been eluding me.

Not that it was difficult. I had just been too busy running away from it.

The hole of emptiness inside me began to fill with a radiance and value far beyond any posturing of my personality. It was enough to be at home in myself. I would not have voluntarily chosen the stripping away that had brought me to this place, and it took several years of unravelling but, resting at last in nothingness helped to show me who I truly am. In its own way, this is the Grace I am talking about.

This is the evidence that life takes care and is always leading us home to ourselves. Yes, it is fierce Grace, but Grace all the same.

Chapter Thirty-Six
Everything is Burning

When one of the biggest fires in the history of California started to blaze a path towards our home, Vinit and I were busy leading our first retreat together.

It was Saturday, September 12, 2015, and the retreat was called, "Becoming Wholly Human," an invitation for participants to shine their spiritual insights on the challenges currently facing our planet, especially climate change. But as we discussed the damage we were inflicting on this fragile, precious planet, as it floated silently through space, a more immediate threat was looming beyond our group room.

On a break, I walked outside for some fresh air and in the distance saw the skies burning orange and flames on far off hillsides. Gradually, I realized they were heading our way, driven by strong winds.

Vinit and I had moved here two years previously, purchasing a house in Hidden Valley Lake, not far from Harbin Hot Springs, a community which came the closest to the commune life that I knew, where we could be free and naked and real with each other. It was our home and also our new playground.

Here, we were able to offer workshops and retreats, combining our qualities as facilitators, with my skill in working with the inner psyche and Vinit's understanding of the ecological and social issues we are dealing with on the Planet.

At first, the threat from the fire did not seem real. My biggest concern occurred when our cook called and told us she couldn't make it to the retreat, because of the fire, and I was wondering what we were going to eat for dinner.

We sat and watched as the fire grew closer, hoping that the wind direction would change, or the fire department would arrive to extinguish it. But when neither of these things happened and embers started flying through the air and hitting our house, things got very scary, very fast.

Red Sky

With the internet down and no access to news, Vinit and I decided we would have to evacuate. The wall of flames was now all around us and we could not recommend any guaranteed escape route for our participants. We just said goodbye, wished them well and prayed they would be safe.

After that, we ran through the house, collecting our cat and various items to load into the car, not knowing if our house would be spared, or if we would lose everything.

The sky was dark at 4:00 p.m. There was fire, smoke, and ash everywhere and hurricane-like winds were whipping the flames along. I had never been through a natural disaster or been confronted with loss and devastation on such a scale.

So many lives were impacted so suddenly, unexpectedly, and irrevocably.

As the fire spread across 80,000 acres, destroying the houses and towns in its path, an old familiar pain started burning inside me. I began to feel a sense of loss on a deeper level. An abyss opened within me, triggering that old, old wound of being alone and afraid, and without the loving presence of my mother, never being able to feel at home.

Living in the Hidden Valley area, embraced by the local community, soothed by the healing waters of Harbin Hot Springs, I had dared to hope that I'd found a place where I belonged. Finally, I could come home to myself.

But the wildfire had other ideas. It raged through the neighborhood, scorching everything in its red-hot fury, leaving nothing behind.

The sacred trees, the land, many of our friends' homes… the whole community was shattered and scattered. Harbin itself was completely destroyed.

Although our home was spared, my heart went out to those who had lost theirs, and the aftermath of the fire was a gut-wrenchingly mournful time. I was heartbroken to see our beloved Harbin torched to the ground, and the community shattered.

But it was also a time of great kindness and generosity. Like others who had been spared by the fire, we gave tents and sleeping bags to the homeless, we cooked meals for them, we helped at the temporary campsites set up to house the homeless.

Fierce Grace

In extreme moments such as these, there is a fierce and tender grace that shines through tragedy, a simple and abiding love, expressing itself in many ways, such as:

"I am so glad you are alive!"

"We've lost everything, but we still have each other!"

"I'm so grateful I found my cat."

"Thank God you still have your home."

I was deeply moved by the love and care everyone showed for each other during this distressing time. The resilience of the community showed in our willingness to support each other, and the experience bonded us all.

The local supermarket gave out IOUs so people could shop and feed themselves and their families. Everyone donated whatever they could, emptying out their closets for clothes, cleaning out pantries for food. This was the upside of the disaster: the goodness of people's hearts.

In a quiet moment, I sat in the garden under the full moon with my girlfriend Linda, who had lost everything. Thoughtfully, she said, "Now I can see the moon so much more clearly."

In her wise way, she was acknowledging how she felt set free as she watched the fire burn everything she possessed; her own home and four rental houses she had owned in the area. Always resilient and resourceful, she soon focused on rebuilding her life for her family.

But strangely, I did not recover as easily as some of the fire's victims. Even though I had four secure walls surrounding me, and my beloved beside me in a warm bed at night, a sense of dread pervaded me.

The fire had reminded me, once again, that there is no permanent state of security, that everything I want to rely on can be snatched away at any moment. As the Irish poet John O'Donohue says, we never really recover from the shock of being born here on this plane of existence, and our journey through life consists of constant challenges.

The noted Buddhist teacher, Chogyam Trungpa, puts it another way, "The spiritual journey is one insult after another."

And the Buddhist teachings to which I was increasingly drawn say that Impermanence is one of the characteristics that we need to face in life if we want to wake up. Life is constantly changing, and nothing stays the same.

I know that's only half the story. But sometimes it's the only half I can see. And the darkness through which I viewed my world was about to get a whole lot darker.

Chapter Thirty-Seven
The Last Time

"I'm going to Spain for a yoga training," I said to my father. "I'll be staying there for a week. But I'll be back in a heartbeat if you need me."

My father lay frail and tired in his bed. He looked at me with sad eyes.

"I don't know what to do," he said. I didn't know what he meant. I thought he meant he was afraid we were going to put him in a home.

"You're going to be fine, Dad, totally fine." I tried to reassure him, aware of my own unwillingness to feel his fear and uncertainty. I didn't even consider that he could be dying.

My dad, the only dad I had ever known, had been a mother to me as well as a father. My spiritual friend, my lifelong companion. He had been my everything. I could not face the fact that he might be dying. So, I closed my eyes and ears, shuttered my heart, and carried on regardless.

I left him then, after wrestling with the decision to go or not to go. I discussed it with Graham, who lived only ten minutes away and was there to shop and cook for my dad regularly, but he had a big gig in Germany scheduled that he could not cancel. He urged me to stay as Dad was declining. I weighed up my needs, wants, and desires against my dads unspoken need for me to stay. And of course, my needs won, as they always did. I always was a willful one. And where was I going, after all, on my endless quest for freedom and experience? Nothing ever fulfills this quest, nothing in the world ever does.

Here I was again, running from pain and chasing after pleasure, in the name of Freedom. As the Buddha once said, the root cause of suffering is attachment and desire.

Chasing Dreams

Dad taught me many things over his lifetime. In his final lesson, like the master he was, he taught me that chasing after dreams and desires and running from pain is futile. To be here now was the most important thing we could give ourselves, and those we love. Nothing we do on the outside really makes a difference. It is our simple love, expressed through being present with those whom we love, that brings true happiness. I won't get another chance to spend those moments with him, sharing tenderness, love, and care. But I know I will remember this lesson for as long as I live.

The decision to head to Spain for a yoga retreat was a hard one. Yet I had no idea how much I would regret this decision, which took precedence over his small aching, heartfelt, statement, "I don't know what to do." He didn't say directly, "Don't go." He was too proud and undemanding to say that, but if I had been listening, I would have heard him begging me silently.

Before I left, we took one last walk together in the park on the green grass of England. My aging father was almost blind, and partially deaf. We trod together slowly across the grass. It was a ritual we'd had for years: we would take off our shoes, and like little children we would delight in feeling the soft grass slipping between our toes. Looking around, I imagined I was my father's eyes, seeing the beauty of a willow tree, its long branches wafting in the air, and a tall sycamore hosting scampering squirrels. Spring was here and the bird song at sunset was like an angelic choir. The sky was ever changing in its beauty and mysteriousness: one moment clouds, the next, blue skies, the next, a brood of floating white cotton balls, dancing like damsels across the aerial landscape.

A black dog tore across the meadow chasing a ball as though this was the first time it had ever been thrown. Children squealed and screamed their happy cries of delight, playing together in the kids' play area, totally absorbed in their world of wonder while parents looked on, absorbed in their own adult cares and concerns. How blessed I felt to sense, to see, and to hear all this, the multi-faceted wonder of everyday life. I imagined what it was like not to have a body to experience all this.

Departed Friends

As I walked with my father, I recalled my friend Shuchi, who had died a few years earlier. A massive brain tumor took her out within a few days. The sad irony was that she'd just gotten back from having a facelift in Mexico. She looked so beautiful on her deathbed, like an angel, so pure, so young, and radiant. Her eyes were open, but, of course, she wasn't there to see through them. I hated that my dear friend had gone in her prime, leaving us so suddenly. I still have her poetry, written as if from beyond, reminding us what a miracle this life is, and how not to take any of it for granted; we need to savor each precious moment.

I had another young friend, who also died while in her prime. Disha, beloved of so many sannyasins, she was a singer, songwriter, lover of life and spirit. She bled to death in the middle of the night in Australia, after the doctor had told her to go home, that her pain was probably just stomach cramps. The ectopic pregnancy burst her ovaries and she died on the floor in agony as her darling man held her tenderly in his arms. The strange thing was that Disha, although only in her early thirties, had already written her own eulogy and prepared everything for her death and funeral. In it, she reminded us that she had loved every moment of this precious life., and that we shouldn't grieve for her.

And then there was Zeno, my outrageous friend. I can still see her olive skin and dark laughing eyes framed by her long dark hair. She was always late, as she was so busy being in the present moment with whomever she was with, or whatever she was doing. And one day, she followed on behind as everyone else went walking in the Himalayas, close to Manali. She didn't come home that night, and the next day a search party found her at the bottom of a ravine, broken, bruised, and very dead.

All We Have

We have no idea how, when, or what will be the conditions of our demise. We know only that this moment is all we have. And it will be over all too soon. I mused on all the friends I have lost to death as I walked on the green grass holding my dad's frail hand. I had not realized how fragile my father was, how much he needed me as he got older, and that I was the one who could have taken care of him. My brother Graham was there in London only ten minutes away, doing all he could but working hard as an artist to get gigs and make money. I was far away on the other side of the ocean, only coming every few months to visit him.

My father had been an advocate of health and fitness his whole life, doing many practices, diets and exercises to keep his body healthy and youthful. Even up to the end he would go to the gym three times a week.

About ten years before he died—when he was in his late seventies—my father had a stroke in his sleep. He was living in Italy with his very young girlfriend in an old stone farmhouse outside a medieval village. It was wintertime. When he awoke one morning he couldn't speak. His girlfriend called the hospital, and the municipality came and dug through the snow to take him in for medical care. Even though it had been many hours since the stroke, he was fortunate to have survived without major damage to his brain or body. Luckily, he still had full mobility and was able to regain his speech, although his brain was slower, and he struggled with his words. That was the first step in his decline. And still, I didn't see his need, his fragility and aging. And perhaps neither did he.

Chapter Thirty-Eight
Twilight

My father continued traveling, spending his winters in Thailand. I met him there once around that time. Dad was happiest in the tropics, basking in the sun, his skin bronzed and tanned and his handsome face wrinkled but healthy looking.

He was enjoying this heavenly place, stepping out from his room each morning to spend long lazy days on the beach with the sound of the ocean lapping against the shore, getting massages from the lovely Thai ladies.

Each morning we would meet in the meditation hall of the local spa for a 7:00 a.m. meditation. And then, one morning, after the meditation, he turned to me and said with concern, "I can't see anything. I've gone blind."

"What do you mean, Dad?" I asked in disbelief. "How can that have happened so suddenly?"

But it was true. I now had to hold my father's hand so he could navigate the walk along the beach or cross the road to his favorite Thai restaurant; trips which just a day or so before he had been quite capable of making alone.

I was shocked at the sudden change in my father's reality, but I was thankful I was there to take him back to London, and that I could help him get settled. I really had no comprehension of how it is to suddenly lose your sight from one moment to the next. To not be able to see the ocean, the sunrise, or the sunset, which you had seen only the day before.

The Vulnerability of Aging

In London, we learned he had "AMD," which stands for age-related macular degeneration. His retinas had been deteriorating for some time, a process most likely accelerated by the sun, which he loved to lay in without sunglasses.

It was only now, as I struggle with the same condition, that I understand the vulnerability of losing your sight, and how much we rely on our eyes to help us navigate through the world.

After seeing him settled back in England, I returned to America, but traveled back and forth to see him as often as I could.

He also came to visit me in the United States several times and was there to attend my wedding—the last time he would come. He was slowing down. His mental capacities were declining, his sight had gone, and his hearing was bad.

I used to ask him, "How're you doing Dad?"

"From the neck down, I'm doing great!" he would reply dryly with a chuckle.

The last trip we took together was a family vacation in Ireland. My father was excited to visit Ireland, where he had spent a chunk of his childhood.

I know it meant a lot to him to show us the green, green land that he loved and the home he had grown up in with his brothers and sisters. But ever in the role of caretaker, I found it hard to relax and enjoy those precious moments with him.

My obsessive caretaking and need to organize everything made me impatient with his slowness. My restless nature had me keeping us on the go, never really relaxing into my father's snail pace.

Now that I've become all too aware of my own aging body, I regret that. Now that I have the same eye condition, I can

194

finally understand what it means to be slowly losing your sight, and be so helpless, to not even be able to read or write or watch T.V, or dialing a number to call someone on the phone. Even making oneself a cup of tea or a meal is not possible,

Our Last Walk

My heart aches as I think of him that morning in London when we went for that walk in the park. I never could have guessed it would be our last walk together. He shuffled along, slower than ever, but confident about walking across the grass to the bench on the other side of the park.

As always, I walked ahead and stopped to turn to wait for him, or go back and meet him where he was, and then I'd march on ahead again. I've always been that way, quick and fast, the "Makukorba" of my childhood nickname, striding out ahead. As we got halfway across the park, a slight incline in the grass had him struggling and he gasped for breath.

By the time we reached the bench, his thin legs were buckling underneath him, and he sat down heavily, just wanting to go home. I rushed to get the gardeners, who helped him on the long walk home, all 100 yards of it. It took almost an hour for us to reach dad's front door and they had to carry him like a baby over the threshold to lay him on the bed, where he curled himself up into a fetal position.

It's hard to believe now that I could have left him like that. My beautiful, humble, kind father. He had needed me. But I couldn't see it. I was in denial of death and the fact that he didn't have long.

After our walk, I made Dad a meal. I encouraged him to eat but he had no interest in food. I had never seen my father like this. Only two months previously he had been more robust: we had walked in the park and sat in the pub with Graham and talked about going to the Lake District in the summer.

Now he was so much older and more shriveled than I had ever seen him. His body leaned to one side and the arm affected by the stroke dangled awkwardly as he shuffled from the bed to the table to eat a few bites, and then lay back down on the bed with a groan.

It would take him several hours to finish even a simple bowl of porridge, about the easiest food to eat, and which I would gobble down in five minutes before rushing off to the next thing in my busy day.

On a practical level, I took care of things before my departure, shopping for food supplies, arranging medical care and social services, but what he most needed was my loving bedside presence to ease his fears and sit with him in the darkness of the lonely hours left to him as he approached his death.

I Didn't Know

Without sight, no TV could keep him company, and with failing hearing and only a few brain cells left after the stroke, there was no activity with which he could occupy himself. He used to lie listening to classical music and the hourly news on BBC radio, the "beep—beep—beep" marking the top of the hour when the news headlines would come on.

Now he had no interest in music or news. I cannot imagine what went on inside of him in the long hours of the day, as it stretched into another endless night of aloneness.

Sleep evaded him and the twilight hours of the night stretched before him as he began to slip away from this world. Finally, I hugged him, made sure he was comfortable. And then I left.

In my week away, while I was stretching and opening my body, learning more about yoga and the liberation of the mind through meditation, my father lay languishing in ever increasing pain, inner turmoil, and torture in his dark world.

I talked with him every day. He told me he couldn't sleep, and I empathized and encouraged him to get some sleeping pills. I had no idea how bad he was, or maybe I didn't want to know.

When I called one morning and he did not pick up as usual, I panicked that something had happened to him. I called my brother.

"Graham? Where's dad?" I asked, worried out of my mind.

"He's had a fall," Graham said, his voice calm and matter of fact. "He's at the hospital. He is okay, just shaken up."

My tense shoulders relaxed, and I breathed a sigh of relief to know he was still alive. He'd just had a fall; nothing too serious. I flew back to London, not able to get there fast enough. I rushed to the hospital to find my father very confused.

He didn't know what was going on. He had a lot of pain in his bladder and trouble peeing. This had been going on for a while, but now it was worse. I didn't realize this was the last time I would see my father conscious enough to be able to speak.

After a while, my father opened his eyes. "I'm so glad you came," he said, his voice nearly a whisper. "I thought you had left it too late."

He clasped my hand, his diminished strength trying so hard to hold me. I was stricken with remorse and sorrow that I had not been there for my father when he needed me. I was too busy, always going somewhere, other than right here, where I was needed.

The lesson for me was to get out of my own way and my own agenda, to see what was right in front of me, and what was needed in the moment.

Life was always talking to me. But I was too busy with my plans and personal preoccupations. I couldn't see the reality before my eyes.

Fumbling towards Freedom / Rajyo Allen

Chapter Thirty-Nine
Death Changes it all

My father never came home from the hospital. The infection he developed turned out to be a cancerous growth in his bladder, with many complications. Despite excellent care and all the treatment they could give him, in his weakened state he declined rapidly. He didn't want to be here anymore. To go on living in this decrepit body with only a few of his faculties was a miserable existence for this once vibrant and alive being. He wanted to go.

Still, I could not believe he was dying. My father had been invincible. He did everything to take care of his health and stay young and fit. He always thought he could cheat aging and death. He had not let the stroke stop him, nor had his blindness defeated him. He moved slower, of course, but he never let these things stop him. He would lie in bed telling me about the next book he wanted to write. How could he possibly die? I just could not believe that my father would leave this world...leave me. I wanted him to be here forever, strong and steady in my life as the one certain thing. Wherever I had gone wandering, he had always been there upon my return, his arms wide open.

Even when he was older, I could ask him how to get somewhere in London and he would tell me which underground tubes to take and which stations to change at. He always knew the way; when I was lost, he was my guide

He had been the inspiration for my spiritual path, bringing me up on Gurdjieff's teachings. Our paths had intertwined constantly throughout my life. He had introduced me to Osho. And he later followed me on that path, being initiated into Sannyas twelve years after me.

For Whom the Bell Tolls

The clock on the wall in his hospital room had stopped. Now it said 8:00 when it was really 4:00. Then it said 2:00 when it was really 6:00. It made no sense. At home in his flat, in the night, empty now without his presence, I heard the church bells chime. They also didn't keep time. There was no time that added up to what those church bells were chiming.

"They must be tolling for him," I thought.

We were in a timeless zone, waiting, watching, waiting. Time became irrelevant, meaningless. I hated time. I wished I could turn back the clocks and buy more time. But for my father, time was slipping away.

I was in denial of sickness and death. How could my daddy leave me? How was I going to live without him? I was, as usual, thinking of my own needs. I hadn't been aware that this beautiful beloved man also needed me. I was his lifeline. Even from a young age, he'd always called me his angel. But I didn't save him, and I could not save him now.

I remembered the way he would shuffle down the hall to greet me when I would arrive back home, weary traveler that I was, with my room always waiting for me. How he would send me off again, waving at the door when I would leave on another trip—who knows where—going to find what I thought I was looking for.

Dear Old Dad

All I really wanted was home, and the unconditional undying love of my dear old dad, the one who brought me up and sacrificed so much for me when his wife, my mother, had died.

We watched his body decline. The meds stopped working, and the doctors took him off active treatment, giving him only morphine to stop the pain. I couldn't believe I was watching him slip away from this life, away from me.

Graham and I sat by his bedside and watched his body shutting down. His beautiful blue eyes rarely opened any more. He could no longer make conversation or hear what we were saying to him. I said goodbye to my daddy, trying to let him know what a wonderful father he had been, and what a great friend, teacher, and fellow traveler, he was. As the day came when it was time to say our final goodbyes, we were told we could sleep in the hospital if we wished, to be near him, to be close. I went home to sleep, again thinking he would be there the next day, as he had always been.

I got the call early next morning. A nurse told me my father didn't have very long. I rushed to the hospital. In the taxi on the radio, I heard Joni Mitchell's voice singing, "Don't it always seem to go that you don't know what you got 'til it's gone." How poignant and relevant. In the middle of early morning London traffic, the tears fell down my face for the loss of my beloved father. The world outside the window seemed very grey and colorless. By the time I arrived he was already gone. His body looked peaceful, but far from us. I could not believe he was dead. I was stunned and amazed that this had all happened so fast. It was better for him, that he was here and then gone in the blink of an eye, that was how he would have wanted it.

But how was I going to live without him? I see him everywhere; his presence is all around me. But I can't talk to him anymore, can't see his beautiful face or wash his lovely feet.

Beautiful Soul

I have experienced this before when friends leave the body, and Osho, too. How their presence is so pervasive, and the fragrance of their soul perfumes the air everywhere. But never had I so keenly felt the physical absence of someone I loved.

I have so much gratitude for all my father gave me, this beautiful soul who blessed my life in so many ways. You have

201

taught me so much, Daddy, please infuse me with your courage, your passion, your patience, your acceptance, your sweet surrender to life, your free spirit, and your magnificent soul.

Suddenly the damned clock has started working again and we are not waiting anymore. He has gone, gone, gone beyond. The Buddhist mantra played in my head constantly:

"Gate, Gate, Para Gate, Parasamgate, Bodhi Swaha".

"Gone, gone, gone beyond, gone totally beyond. Oh, what an awakening!"

I prayed that his passion for truth and love and freedom was carrying him into the light and towards a fortunate rebirth.

We sat with him for hours, praying, meditating, and sending him on his way. I told him all the things for which I was grateful. Then we washed his beautiful, wasted body.

Thank you, my love, for the beautiful life you lived, for all you gave to so many. For your courage and trust and sense of adventure. And for your sweet surrender to life and death.

A short while after my father left his body, I had a dream. Actually, it was more like a visitation from him, as I can still remember it as clearly as if it happened yesterday. My father and I were driving along in the countryside. I dropped him in a beautiful place with green meadows, sunshine and bird song. There were dancing girls all around. He was wearing monk's robes and he was completely relaxed and joyful…

My father waved goodbye in my dream as I drove off to get gas. At the gas station, suddenly I had to take a poop. I looked around and as no one was there I pooped on the gas station floor. The gas station attendant came along and asked me what I was doing. "I am cleaning up my shit" I replied, somewhat embarrassed. Ain't that the truth! My father is in the heavenly realms and I am here on Earth, cleaning up my karma!

Chapter Forty
A New Home

While I was in Europe with my dying father, my husband, Vinit was trying to find us a new home after the fires had devastated our area. So, I was living in two worlds at once, with my father in London, and with Vinit in California. What a bizarre juxtaposition.

I wanted to tell Vinit "Drop it, we'll do that later. Let me be here now, with this passage of my father." But faced with Vinit's sense of urgency to leave the devastated area of Hidden Valley Lake, I didn't have the will to protest.

Vinit called me one morning, his voice choked with emotion, saying, "I've found our new home, honey. It's so perfect for us, and you're gonna love it!"

"Really?" I said cautiously, "Are you sure it's right for us?"

I asked him all kinds of questions to clarify if it had everything we were looking for. He kept reassuring me, how much I would love it, and I could feel his desire to make me happy, but the nagging feeling of doubt in my gut kept saying, "This is not right, this is not meant to be."

Vinit was so excited, and I was so overwhelmed with the situation in London that I said, "If you feel it's right, I trust you." And he began the process of buying it.

The house was located in Sebastopol, a small town in Sonoma County, the heart of California's wine country, with vineyards everywhere. It was supposed to be a fashionable place to live, but as we drove down the shaded country lane towards the house, I had serious misgivings. Something about it just didn't feel right.

Nothing is Right

Pulling up in the driveway, I looked at the hexagonally shaped house and could see why Vinit fell in love with it. Never one for straight lines and conventional shapes, Vinit had fallen for the unusual design of the house. The front door was around at the back of the house, which according to the Chinese art of Feng Shui is not a good idea. But there was a bunch of flowers waiting for me at the door, with a note saying, "I welcome you, my Queen, to your new palace. May you be very happy here in your new home."

Vinit picked me up and carried me over the threshold. I was touched by his sincere desire to make me happy in our new home and managed to give him a weak smile. I did not love the house as he did. Maybe it was my state of mind and heavy heart, still grieving for my father, but somehow everything felt wrong and out of place.

Nevertheless, I gave it my best shot. Vinit and I got busy with remodeling and painting, moving the front door to where it should be—at the front of the house—taking down walls, putting up walls, and doing our best to make it a lovely home; it turned out to be beautiful. Our neighbors were welcoming at first, but their friendliness waned as they endured construction noise and the frequent arrival of friends and visitors.

There was something else on my mind: When I had held my father's hand, as he lay dying in hospital, it seemed to me that I received a silent message from him that I should get a dog, and that somehow his spirit would be with me in the animal. So, when a friend called me on my birthday to say that two cockapoo puppies were looking for a nice loving home, I became excited, went to see them, and fell in love with them. It felt like a sign from my father.

Cockapoo is a special breed, crossbred from a cocker spaniel and a poodle. Their soft tan fur and the soulfulness of their big brown eyes melted my frozen heart. I could not bear to leave one of them behind, so I came home with both. I named the stockier, cheekier puppy, Ricky, after my father. The more timid, sensitive pup we named Rama, after the Hindu God. They became part of our big family, along with three other housemates, and a bunch of interesting characters who were helping us remodel the house.

Welcome to the Madhouse

It was crazy, with construction going on from early morning until late evening, workers and housemates constantly on the move, and the puppies barking, messing, and escaping into the forest to run wild chasing the deer. There was no peace.

Even though we were living at the end of a remote, small country road, difficult for large numbers of people to access, we decided to push ahead with our dream of creating a retreat center. It was a mad idea and Vinit and I had misgivings about it, that we unfortunately didn't heed. But we started converting and extending the garage to create a group room and we turned the huge third floor of the house into a large dormitory.

The neighbors, who had initially been welcoming and friendly, began to object and created trouble. They reported us to the county, and the county came down on us for zoning violations. We had to take down the beautiful teepee in the garden and modify the in-law unit we had created. Of course, there was nothing we could do to hide the massive group room we had created, into which we had poured all our finances.

When the neighbors and the county became hostile, this started to seriously affect Vinit's state of mind. He started freaking out, imagining that there would be serious consequences for violating the zoning laws and he became more and more anxious, pacing the house all night, and not eating during the day. I watched my husband slowly lose his mind. After weeks of not sleeping, he was in a paranoid and delusional state. I had no idea how to convince him of reality: yes, the neighbors were giving us a hard time, but it wasn't the end of the world. He was convinced they were ganging up on us and that we might end up in jail.

Fumbling towards Freedom / Rajyo Allen

Chapter Forty-One
Off to the Asylum

Over lunch at a restaurant in town, a friend convinced Vinit to go to a psychiatric clinic for an evaluation, which he agreed to do.

When the staff psychiatrist asked him if he was having thoughts of killing himself, he said that he had been feeling hopeless and wasn't sure if he wanted to go on. She then informed him that they were keeping him in. The first I heard about this was when he called and asked me to bring his washbag, as he was being held there and he didn't know how long it would be.

When I walked into the place, I was shocked to see Vinit in an institutionalized lock up. Fluorescent lights, cold steel, and glass...and overweight uptight security guards in uniforms.

I saw Vinit with other people in various states of mental disarray. How could this be happening to my normally stable and buoyant husband? They took away anything that he could use to kill himself: belts, pens, dental floss. He was in seriously deep doo-doo now, and I could not take him home.

From this clinic, he was sent to a mental institution and into a ward for seriously psychotic inmates, the real loonies. There were dangerously deranged people in there. Vinit continued to freak out. He was going downhill fast, had no grip on reality and he was surrounded by people who were seriously mentally ill.

I was in shock at the speed with which, in an apparently free and democratic society, an ordinary person could be thrown into a lockup with a bunch of certified crazies.

Delusional

Fortunately, we managed to get him out of that ward, and into another, where attendance was mostly voluntary. Vinit's prison was mainly inside his own head, but he was confined to this place too, with nothing to do except listen to the TV blaring incessantly and watch the minutes of the clock ticking endlessly by. Time crawled along until the next institutionalized meal was served.

Every time I visited him, once and often twice a day, he would look as dejected and hopeless as ever. He would say to me, "It's too late, I know I'm going to be sent to the Napa Sanitarium, where they keep people forever." Nothing I could say could convince him otherwise, nor could he convince the staff that he was getting better. It was not a good situation.

At home, I was dealing with the crisis with the neighbors and realizing that after spending a fortune on this property, the only sensible thing to do was to cut our losses and sell the house, thereby relieving Vinit's anxiety.

Fortunately for Vinit, his family had the means to help him, and they pulled out the big guns to get him transferred to an expensive facility in Arizona that used cutting-edge therapies as well as drugs to treat their patients. I went to stay close to him for a month while he went through the program.

Bouncing Back

It took three weeks of careful medication and plenty of skilled support before Vinit was able to turn the corner. From then on, he made a miraculous recovery and started returning to his old carefree self. He told me how grateful he was and how much compassion he now had for the victims of trauma and addiction who suffer from mental illness.

He bounced back and began to lead the weekly talent show, staged by recovering patients in the facility, and also began to counsel others in the program.

By the end of the month, Vinit was fully back and before Christmas we were able to go home. I was overjoyed to have my man back to his normal happy self, laughing and joking with me.

Shortly before his return, I asked him what he would need in order to look forward to coming home.

He replied: "I need to know that the situation of the house has been remedied. We need to make all the modifications legal."

Fortunately for us, AJ, our wonderful contractor, managed to do some quick alterations and pull some bureaucratic strings so that, within a short time, the county had no red flags against us.

A Heartbreaking Choice

"And I need you to give up the puppies," Vinit went on. "They are just too crazy for me. I don't think I can handle it."

I was in shock.

"Noooo!" I silently argued. "Please don't ask me to give up the puppies. That's the one thing that gives my life meaning, and Ricky is my connection to my father!"

But I knew Vinit's condition was shaky. I would have to choose between my husband's sanity and my darling puppies, who had been the source of so much love and joy for me. Ricky was my dog, and it really did feel as though I could connect to my father through him. We had such a bond. I couldn't bear the thought of losing that connection.

But I had to choose my husband, and I had to let go of the puppies. It broke my heart. After saying goodbye to my father, parting with those dogs was one of the hardest things I have ever done in my life. Ricky, darling Ricky!

For a while, I tried to hang onto him. I plotted and planned to see how I could keep both, but Vinit was too fragile to have any disturbance and I could not risk triggering another breakdown.

Fortunately, we found good homes for the puppies, where they were loved and happy, and I visited them for walks.

Each time, my heart would be ripped open, as Ricky would leap all over me, so thrilled to be with me again. He and I were so connected.

Having just lost my dad, I had almost lost my husband, and now I had to say goodbye to my puppies... on top of losing our home. It was all too much, and my heart was on the ground. What more would it take to learn this lesson of impermanence?

Chapter Forty-Two
Himalayan Healing

With my father gone and Vinit restored to his stable self, it was time for us to do something completely different. We both needed a break.

Together, Vinit and I boarded a plane for the mystic East in the form of a trip to Tibet. It was a place I had dreamed about visiting for many years, especially Lhasa, this holiest of cities for the Tibetan people.

I have always felt such deep empathy and compassion for the peaceful Tibetan people who were so violently taken over by the Chinese and have since been subjugated and persecuted by the Chinese government.

I had made three previous attempts to visit Tibet but each time my body had not been strong enough to endure the high altitude of that country.

This time, I was determined, and I hoped that being with these brave people would somehow help me overcome the endless grief I was feeling.

I sensed that somehow the Tibetans could teach me about non-attachment and impermanence, core principles of Gautam Buddha's teachings, which I sorely needed.

We landed in Kathmandu and spent a few days there to acclimatize to the high altitude before heading into Tibet.

I was saddened to see this once beautiful city now overrun with cars and full of pollution and noise.

I remembered the times I had sat with hippies and lepers at the temples in Durbar Square, watching cows and people wandering slowly by, in an atmosphere of peace and spaciousness, surrounded by the stillness of the majestic mountains one could see in the distance.

Earthquake Devastation

But even more shocking was the devastation caused by the Gorkha Earthquake, which had shaken Nepal a couple of years earlier, in April 2015. It had killed almost 9,000 people, leaving hundreds of thousands of people homeless, and it had damaged or destroyed centuries-old buildings, including those in Durbar Square, where several temples were cracked, crumbling or in ruins.

I was horrified to see my beautiful Nepal so ravaged, but I was also fearful of what we might encounter in Tibet, knowing we were heading into Chinese territory. I searched my cell phone and luggage for any evidence of the Dalai Lama or affiliation with the Tibetans.

I dearly wanted to take some gifts or memorabilia to the people there, reminding them of the days when they could freely show their devotion to their spiritual leader, the Dalai Lama. But I couldn't risk it. I knew there were severe penalties for any "seditious" activities. So, I slunk through the security and was grateful I was not caught for anything.

We stayed in a large traditional Tibetan hotel for our first three days in Lhasa, acclimatizing to the rarified air.

Even walking was an effort and climbing staircases was tiring.

As for the Tibetans, they were loving and kind, but I could sense the burden of repression hanging over them. They were not free to say or do as they wish due to constant surveillance by the Chinese.

Inspiration

Yet many of those I met had light hearts and high spirits. As far as I could see, they were less identified with events on the physical plane. They know everything is transitory.

It was a reminder to me that identification and attachment create suffering.

I could see how much suffering I had created for myself in my life because I have held on tightly to other people, to my self-image, and to my ideas about how the world should be.

The Tibetan people seemed to be living more in the moment, with open hearts and quiet minds, not obsessing about the past or future.

When we walked the *kora* around the Potala—the Dalai Lama's palace—I was happy to see devout Tibetans prostrating themselves on their hands, knees, and bellies, practicing their faith, uncaring of who was watching them.

I tried to imagine what it had been like here when these people were free, honoring the Buddha's philosophy with faith and devotion: Do no harm. Be compassionate and kind to everyone.

Life is impermanent so work tirelessly to become enlightened and to serve others.

What would it be like if the whole world could live the way these people have so sincerely endeavored to live?

Fumbling towards Freedom / Rajyo Allen

Chapter Forty-Three
Pilgrimage to Tibet

After acclimatizing to the high altitude of Tibet, we took off in a chartered bus with a Tibetan guide who spoke English well. He had escaped from Tibet to India but had returned to be with his family.

We travelled around the country, visiting the vast high plains and beautiful monasteries—restored to impress the tourists—where skeleton crews of monks were able to maintain the buildings.

Finally, we arrived at Mount Kailash, considered by many spiritual seekers to be the cosmic center of the universe. I was excited and scared. I knew this trip would be grueling and we would be physically challenged in the harsh conditions surrounding this magnificent mountain. This was the holiest of holies, to Buddhists and Hindus alike, and was said to clear the karma of many lifetimes. I prayed it would do that for me.

Many pilgrims were conducting a *kora* around the mountain, mostly on foot, but some on horseback, and many Tibetans were prostrating themselves on hands and knees all the way around Kailash to gain special merit. They had old shoe soles strapped to their hands and knees and thick leather aprons.

They knelt, prayed, lay down, stretched out, then moved to the spot where their hands had rested, and repeated the gesture. And so, they moved, one body length at a time, around Kailash. I was touched by the single-minded focus of these devout pilgrims, and I prayed for a similar kind of strength to overcome my challenges.

Guru Purnima

I knew I had the opportunity to shed an old skin and be reborn anew, to gain merit from this journey. I had my father's ashes with me, and I wanted to scatter them to the winds from the slopes of Kailash. I felt honored to be with these fellow pilgrims, travelers from many foreign lands and from Nepal, India, and Tibet itself.

Our trip coincided with Guru Purnima, a full moon holiday in July that is sacred to the Hindus, and which we had celebrated with Osho at the ashram in Pune. It brought many pilgrims from far and wide to pay homage at Mount Kailash.

We set off from a town on the plateau where we had been able to stock up on goods that we might need. We had umbrellas to shield us from the sun and all the warm clothes we might need, which were carried for us on horseback. I was grateful I did not have to carry a heavy pack since the mere act of walking and breathing was so demanding. I was glad to know we had supplies of oxygen should they be needed.

The starkness of the landscape was breathtaking. Above the tree line, the prayer flags on the shrines were strung across the mountain sides, blowing in the wind. We said prayers for the cessation of suffering for all beings, and prayers for the liberation of many.

I have always appreciated how the Tibetan Buddhist religion doesn't just seek liberation for the Tibetan people. It encourages us all to follow the path of the Bodhisattva. In their prayers and acts of loving kindness, Buddhists wish for the liberation of all beings, vowing not to leave this place of samsara, the endless cycle of birth and death, until every being is free.

Slowly my heart began to soften and open beyond my own pain and grief. I saw how these noble people who had lost so much could still laugh and enjoy life, while at the same time being kind and compassionate to all.

Grueling Journey

The fact that the journey around the mountain was so challenging also helped me take my attention off myself.

Each night we would stay with the other pilgrims in large tents, where food was cooked, and large quantities of salted Tibetan butter tea were liberally shared.

We ate simple meals of noodles or fried rice and slept on large cot beds covered with beautiful Tibetan rugs that lined the sides of the tents. We would snuggle up for the night to the sound of Tibetans chatting and some people snoring. It was a community event, and all pilgrims were treated as honored guests in these humble surroundings.

When we reached the high mountain village of Zutrulpuk we stopped for the night to prepare to go over the pass. We took a day's rest, as the push over the pass would be challenging. It was a lovely sunny day and I decided to visit a nearby cave, made sacred by the great enlightened yogi, Milarepa, who lived there centuries earlier. Milarepa's words echoed in my head as I was walking, giving me strength and courage to keep going.

"My religion is to live and die without regret," he said. "Toss to the winds your concerns for this life, and impress on your mind the unknown time of your death. Remembering the pain of samsara, why long for the unnecessary?"

We rested, ate, and readied ourselves for an early morning start over the pass. I drew strength and courage from the feeling of being a pilgrim with so many other devotees. Although we were with people from many countries, it was the Tibetans who touched me the most. They were often as poor as rags, with no possessions to their name, living on whatever alms were given to them along the way. We were fortunate in this village to have rooms with real beds. We laid our sleeping bags on them and went to sleep, eager to make it over the pass the next day. We were to be up before dawn and well on our way by first light.

When we awoke the next morning and stepped outside, all around was a blanket of white: snow which had been falling all night. It was magical. But we had to wonder: could we still make it over the pass? We decided to wait and discuss the situation with more experienced guides. I wanted to push on ahead, excited for the adventure. Others said they preferred to be safe, turn around and go back.

This pause gave us the chance to feast on *tsampa* porridge, eggs, and fried rice; we were never sure when the next good meal would be available, and I was happy to wait until the weather improved.

As the snow continued to fall, it was eventually decided that we westerners were not to continue as it would be too dangerous to keep to the path and make it down the other side, which was very steep and dangerous rocks were hidden under the snow. I was disappointed, as the adventurer in me always wanted to complete a journey.

Ashes to the Wind

We trekked back down the mountain the way we had come, going anti-clockwise this time, in the tradition of the ancient Tibetan Bon lineage. Vinit and I found a spot on the banks of a beautiful river, the source of which feeds four major rivers in Asia: the Ganges, the Indus, the Sutlej, and the Brahmaputra. Releasing my father's ashes into the river meant they would flow to all parts of the subcontinent.

As I watched the last remains of my father's physical form drift downriver in the fast-flowing water, I felt freed from my material attachments and felt his spirit with me on the mountain.

"Fly high my love, without any reason. Fly high my love, there's nowhere to go." Softly, I sang the Osho song that we had sung to departed loved ones in the ashram.

On my return from Tibet, I went back to Nepal to help the villagers rebuild their lives after the tragic earthquake had devastated it. It felt good to be of service in this way, knowing how quickly the ground underneath us can give way.

Chapter Forty-Four
Blue Ridge Mountains

Our house in Sebastopol went on the market. We had spent a year trying to convert it into a retreat center and it would take another year to sell it.

I couldn't wait to move. The place had too many sad memories for me. I longed to leave California and the losses I had experienced over the past few years. Moreover, wildfires were becoming an annual occurrence, as climate change rendered Northern California a hotter, drier, and more dangerous place to live. My parched spirit was reflected in the dry brown hills, the disappearing creeks and streams, and the drought season growing ever more intense each year.

I needed a new start. I envisioned fertile green hills, fresh flowing waters, and mountains all around. I began to hear the call to move to Asheville, North Carolina.

As soon as Vinit was feeling better, we went to visit, and I immediately fell in love with the beautiful Blue Ridge Mountains hugging the valley where Asheville lies. The lush green landscape, the flowing creeks, rivers, and waterfalls signaled new life to me. I could feel joy stirring in my heart for the first time in a long time. It reminded me of my childhood growing up in England, although it was much more vast and spacious.

Lying in bed, in our little Airbnb, in Asheville's historic district, I snuggled up to Vinit and said, "This is our place, my love, I can feel it. This is where we are supposed to live."

He groaned beside me. "Oh no, he said. "I know that means we are moving. When you decide something, that is it."

"I haven't felt as strongly about anything in a while," I responded. "I know it is right. You have to trust me on this one."

It was difficult for Vinit. A California boy, living his whole life in the Golden State, he was reluctant to give up all he had known. But I was clear and he, too, somehow knew it was best for us both. He was still dealing with a tremulous state of mind, and I was still grieving over the loss of my father and the puppies.

By the time the Sebastopol house sold, we couldn't wait to leave, having already made an offer on a property that we knew was meant to be ours, where we could build the retreat center of our dreams.

Vinit completed the sale of our California home and closed the deal on our Asheville property and prepared to do a final two-month silent retreat at his beloved Spirit Rock Buddhist retreat center.

Goodbye to India

Meanwhile, I went on a two-month pilgrimage in India. Somehow, I knew this might be the last time I visited the sacred land that had been a mother to me in so many ways, loving me, holding me, giving me wings to fly on my spiritual journey.

I visited Goa, meeting up with my brother, Alima, and many old friends. I went south to Tiruvannamalai and Arunachala, the sacred mountain of the enlightened mystic Ramana Maharshi, where I sat in the sacred cave and listened for guidance. Then I went north to Dharamsala, the place I had lived with the Tibetans so long ago.

Just outside of Dharamsala, there is a sannyasin center was on the banks of a beautiful river surrounded by the majestic Himalayan mountains. Here, I did a twenty-one-day silent retreat; with Alima and many old sannyasin friends, we dove into silence. Instead of being a peaceful and calm retreat, I went through a deep grieving process with my father and a powerful life review. It was a difficult retreat, as I had to look at aspects of myself I didn't want to see, but I felt cleansed and healed afterwards.

This was a perfect launch into my sixtieth birthday, which I celebrated with Alima and other friends in the town of McLeod Ganj. I reflected that this was the completion of my second Saturn return, heralding a new stage of maturity and wisdom for me. How perfect that I should spend it here where my spiritual journey had begun all those years ago.

Then I went to Rishikesh to sit with the Jamaican-English teacher Mooji, who from his awakened perspective, reminded me that resting in the silence of being, nothing can disturb us, and all is well. Life takes care of Life.

Home at Last

I arrived back home in Asheville, weary from two months of traveling and ready to settle. Vinit was still away on his retreat at Spirit Rock, California, so I had all the time and space I needed to "feel into" our new home.

As I drove up the long driveway, it felt so different from the dark lane in Sebastopol, where I had experienced such a sense of fear and foreboding. Here, the driveway seemed more like a stairway to heaven. As I stood and looked out at the land, I knew this is the place I want to live the rest of my life. And die here.

There were two houses, one in which we were going to live, and one that would become a rental. They stood on solid ground, with ample parking for visiting friends and guests. The beautifully landscaped gardens opened to green meadows, surrounded by forests bordering the property. This was the place I could call home and could finally begin creating our retreat center

Our neighbors were friendly, ready to welcome us, even though, with their strong southern drawl, I barely understood a word they said.

I felt hugged by the land and welcomed by the community. I was surprised to find that everyone in this locality felt like my tribe, my people, aligning with my own free spirit values. The people here have time and space to connect and be present. They are progressive, conscious, and caring, with a real sense of community.

Walking around the interior of our new house, I could easily imagine how each room would be decorated and furnished. My love for creating beauty with use of color and placement of objects was reigniting my passion.

Through all the challenges and pain, I could see how Grace was operating in my life. It conspired to make sure we moved out of California and guided us here. It helped restore my faith in guidance from the beyond.

The pain and difficulty of the last several years was over now. Here, I could sense a new beginning and a new kind of home, not just around me but also inside me. It was a good feeling. And I was happy at last. But I know that to be truly happy in life we have to find peace, acceptance, and surrender with whatever life brings. The Tibetans have taught me that. When I notice I'm suffering, because I'm holding on, either attached to something, or resisting something, I ask myself, "What is it I need to let go of here?"

I soften my belly, take a deep breath, and open to the present moment.

Jack Kornfield, a prominent Buddhist scholar in the US, talks about his Buddhist teacher in Thailand, Ajan Chah, and how he would go for a walk every day and look into everyone's faces, checking the degree of peace or suffering they were in.

He'd say, "Hmm, suffering today? Huh, must be attached!"

My Father's Voice

One day, while searching through my music library for some teachings to listen to while exercising, I found a recording of my father guiding his students through the archetypes on the Hero's Journey. I was so grateful to hear his voice, as if he were suddenly right here with me, masterful and strong, present, compassionate, and wise.

What I heard him say was, "You were doing the best you could with what you knew at the time." His words entered me like a healing force, spreading their balm over my past and all my "mistakes." I could forgive myself. I could relax and let go of the habit of criticizing myself for not making wiser choices in life. I shed tears of relief and a doorway opened to my father's presence and his eternal love for me.

I could finally accept that all the things I wished I had done differently, the mind game trilogy of "woulda, shoulda, coulda," all happened exactly as they were meant to. This stubborn separate little ego that thinks it is in control, and can direct life, is actually not in the driver's seat.

From the enlightened perspective, it is just life happening, and we are simply instruments in a grand orchestra; we play our various parts in the unfolding of life.

In truth, love is all there is, and things are exactly as they are. The idea of a separate someone, who has individual free will, is the cause of so much of our suffering. It sure has been for me.

To know that I am not the doer of my life, to get out of the way and see how magnificently life is living me, is my deepest understanding.

Letting go, surrendering, opening with a trusting heart to the mysterious play of the divine within, and all around me, gives me access to a much grander scheme of things unfolding.

Chapter Forty-Five
Moving from Self to Soul

When the caterpillar enters the cocoon, it must feel like a kind of death. In the midst of my own metamorphosis, I couldn't see the possibility of transformation.

I didn't know the freedom of the butterfly. I had to go through a lot of unburdening before I could spread my wings and feel the wind carrying me with the lightness of my being.

I had been brought repeatedly to extreme limits of everything I knew and was then asked to let go and step into the unknown, walking in the dark for a while, emerging each time anew.

These were never easy experiences, and they often involved deaths—deaths of people, farewells to places, goodbye to things I loved—as well as deaths of parts of myself.

Then came a rebirth into a new and different experience.

All that running to faraway places, chasing enlightenment and expanded states of consciousness only prolonged the inevitability of what I finally had to do: stop and come face to face with myself.

The finality of losing my father made it clear to me. There was nowhere to run and nowhere to hide.

All my seeking and searching, all the busy-ness and doing-ness, all my identities of who I thought I was, and all the great ideas about what I wanted to do... Death brought me home to myself.

I did a lot of emotional clearing, a lot of meditation, and a lot of just sitting in my own mess, which was the last thing I wanted to do. I wanted to run from it, fix it, change it, get rid of it, be done with it. But I just had to keep groping in the dark.

Darkness is a Gift

I had to befriend darkness. To make it my home. I had no choice but to trust it because it was my reality. It was painful and uncomfortable, but I knew that if anything was going to lead me to inner peace, it would be this.

Spiritual author Jeff Foster calls being depressed a state of "deep rest." And as Rumi says in his book *The Guest House*, we must welcome these inner states—shame, depression, meanness. They are guides from beyond who violently sweep our house empty of its furniture. They are telling us something. They're teachers. And to constantly try to medicate or meditate our way out of it—or run from it all—misses the point.

As the French philosopher, Blaise Pascal, astutely observed, "All of man's troubles come from his inability to sit quietly with himself, alone in a room."

As I groped in the dark, it didn't matter what anybody said by way of consolation or comfort. Nothing helped. There was no life raft onto which I could grab.

As I dove deeper into the blackness, I started to make it my home. In that darkness I experienced the nigredo.

I had to make friends with the death and decay of my old self, to let go into it, seeing all the parts of myself that were dying, watching my identity project crumble.

By sitting with it all, I had to allow something else, something other than me, to come in and begin the transformation.

No amount of self-improvement could help me here. The self-improvement project was over. From this perspective, I could see that all the self-help work had been completed through my own will. It was my own ego trying to improve itself.

I remembered all the personal growth workshops I had done with great gurus of success like Anthony Robbins, who told the group, "You can change your life!"

That's true on the level of the personality, or ego identity. But I began to understand that real transformation is very different.

We cannot "do it." I began to see that in my undoing, in the unravelling of all that I had known about myself, something else had been happening to me.

Alchemy of Awakening

I call it alchemy, and it has its own way of working. I had to let the alchemy awaken me in its own way. It was no longer about me imposing my will on life. It was about relaxing and embracing what Jesus says: "Thy Will be Done."

A whole different level of surrender and trust was happening. As much as I could feel myself wanting to be in control, I chose instead deep relaxation, surrender, and with this came acceptance of all that I had experienced.

I love the stories of people who speak from that place inside themselves. I think about Nelson Mandela, or the Dalai Lama, and the beauty of their brave hearts, broken open with wisdom and compassion born of their personal suffering.

Or, Eckhart Tolle, when he said, "That's enough. I cannot live with myself (and the suffering of the mind) anymore." That's when he awoke to the vast reality he calls the Eternal Now, full of grace and benediction. Even homeless, sitting on a park bench, he was completely happy and fulfilled.

And what is suffering after all? Buddha said that life is suffering. What did he mean? I believe he meant that when we are identified with a separate sense of self, full of craving and aversion, then life is suffering.

Osho, on the other hand, said that life is a celebration. What did he mean? He was living at the other end of the spectrum, telling us not to identify with that separate sense of self that suffers, but to come to know our true nature, our essence, to live from the heart, in joy and love and celebration. Then everything is a magical holy dance, and we are one with this glorious, magnificent creation. In living fully, we can also embrace death when it comes, and come to know that there is no separation.

I am more at peace now. For a long time, I tortured myself about finding my purpose and doing valuable work in the world. I so desperately wanted to make my contribution and have people see me as a valuable and worthwhile person.

I didn't feel worthy on the inside, so I tried to create it on the outside.

Now, I have compassion for the one who so desperately needed to prove herself. I am okay being nobody special and being perfectly and absolutely just me, just as I am.

What a relief! I am much quieter, more content, less loud and proud in the world.

All the borrowed identities have been replaced by the rising of a stronger sense of myself inside. This shaky ego identity who was so afraid of being found out to be unworthy of love and recognition, that is not who I am.

It's taken a lot of humbling to reach this place. The word humble comes from "humus" which means being returned to the ground of our being.

I love to bow down and kiss the ground, and remember that I am nothing and nobody, and yet one with everything and everybody. The Ground of Being is my true home.

Ultimate Paradox

It's taken a lot for me to accept the ultimate paradox: I am nothing and at the same time everything. A spiritual friend of mine says, "It takes a lot of courage to be nobody." In this there is ease, there is relaxation, there is freedom.

Disappearing as a separate sense of self, a sense of "Am-ness" arises within. It is not a "me," not an "I," just a flow of life moving through me, living me from the inside out and the outside in.

Osho used to say, "Trust Life, Life is God."

Spiritual teacher Mooji says, "Life takes care of Life."

There is nothing we need to do, most of our doing is just interfering. But to reach this place of being nobody, I had to move through the darkness and face myself with courage, continually reminding the voice of my inner critic to back off.

Jesus is known for saying "Judge ye not," and people think he was talking about judging others, but I am sure he was talking about judging oneself.

So, nowadays, if a tsunami of emotion or a storm of mental activity takes me over, I know the clouds are passing and then they'll be gone. It's not the end of the world, it's just the weather! I am less identified with this person, and this personality.

My soul is witnessing the whole show, mostly with an amused smile.

Through all the waves of my life, the fury and the passion, the having and the not having, the loss and the longing; something has been birthed.

My personality still plays itself out and sure, I still have my neuroses and idiosyncrasies, but I don't take that to be who I am. And I don't take myself so seriously anymore.

There's nothing to fix or change, to do or undo.

I see the comings and goings in the mind, and it's okay. I can rest in emptiness, stay in presence, and let everything be as it is, watching the flow of the river of life moving within and all around me.

Fumbling towards Freedom / Rajyo Allen

Chapter Forty-Six
Bringing it All Back Home

Every day, when I wake up, I sit in meditation.

No matter what is going on in the mind, or in the world, I sit on my cushion and become still and quiet, resting in emptiness, finding the fullness within, taking refuge in silence. Going about my business, doing ordinary things like washing up, or cleaning the house, running the retreat center, tending to the garden, focusing on my writing or being with those I love, there is an atmosphere of simplicity, sweetness, and tenderness.

The great heart of loving kindness and compassion is wide enough to include not only the whole world but also myself. The miracle of love that I feel for my family, my friends, the suffering millions around the world, now includes me. And that is a miracle. It's been a long time coming and it hasn't been easy, but as the Buddha said, "You can search the whole wide world, and you won't find anyone anywhere more deserving of love and kindness than the one sitting right here."

I have been seeking the Kingdom of God for my entire life, and I have now discovered it within me. Osho was right, all those years ago, when he honored me with the name Ma Anand Rajyo "Kingdom of Bliss." At the time, it felt way too regal for me. Most of my life felt like a prison of misery. I thought he had made a mistake. Now I understand. As Jesus once said:

"Seek ye first the kingdom of heaven, and all else will be delivered unto you."

Peace at Last

Now that life has ripped away much of my precious identity and all my plans and dreams and goals, this restless seeking and searching for the Kingdom of Heaven within me has borne fruit.

I have peace in my heart, and love in my life. And truly, all is well. It amazes me that the more I get out of the way, the more miraculously Life unfolds.

As I sit here writing, my cat, Issie (short for Isness), sits on the desk by my computer, and my man is sitting at his desk in his office. My home is warm and cozy, and the retreat center we have created is thriving. Life keeps on unfolding. Life keeps rolling along.

As Mooji says, "Trust Life. God's got this."

My own small separate will is not in control. It never has been. And yet we always have the choice, to be in tune with the endlessly flowing river of life, or to try and fight against it. As the sannyasin song says:

"If you don't fight with life,

Life simply helps you…

Takes you on its shoulder."

It is up to us to fight, or to dance with life. And to really dance, then, as the Sufis say, we need to die before we die, experiencing ourselves beyond the small self as that great flow of life and love eternally expressing itself.

Every day I wake up and feel my father's presence, reminding me to live my life fully, as he did, because it will all be over soon enough.

But for me, these days, living fully does not mean partying hard, getting drunk, flirting, or desperately sucking the juice out of every experience. I've been there and done that.

It has more to do with being fully present with every precious moment of the day, and every precious person in my life, including myself.

One more saying of Jesus: "I and my father in heaven are one."

To heal the separation between my earthly father and me, I needed to discover what it means to live in peace with my heavenly father, or with existence.

When I find that place, there is no separation from him or from anyone. Only love. Pure love. Eternally.

There is no need to go anywhere or do anything. Just being with my breath, with each mysterious moment as it unfolds, is enough.

When the mind gets engaged, I can mourn the mistakes of the past, but now I am more able to relax, take a deep breath and drop into my heart, and see the perfection of the events of my life as they unfolded.

I have asked myself what my work is. What is my contribution to this world? When I become silent inside and listen the answer is very clear: the real work is to wake up, just as Gautam Buddha did 2500 years ago and Jesus Christ did 2000 years ago. Just as George Gurdjieff, Ramana Maharshi, Osho, Eckhart Tolle, and Mooji did in the twentieth century.

As my teacher Miranda reminds me, one awakened soul can ignite thousands of others just by their presence.

The work of the New Man that Osho talked about is to birth a new consciousness on the planet. One that does not divide or separate, does not judge or blame, does not kill or conquer, but lives with all contradictions and dualities, and embodies an essential wholeness. With love as the abiding and overarching truth. So be it.

Fumbling towards Freedom / Rajyo Allen

Epilogue
Letter to My Little Girl

Darling Little One,

Well, who could have told you when you were very young, that you would go through so much in your life?

You came into this world, like all other children, so full of love and joy and innocence. And you were loved by both your mommy and your daddy. You spread light everywhere.

And then life happened, with its knocks and wounds and traumas. When your mama died you forgot that you were loved. And you had to face life alone. You did the best you could.

You couldn't have known this was the beginning of your initiatory journey, through all those rites of passage, those stages of life to pass through.

No little one should have to grow up without the loving guidance of a mother. When she has to, like you, then trauma becomes part of the package.

It is a mystery why life gives us these experiences. Maybe without suffering we would never set out on the journey to find out who we are.

You went on a pilgrimage to try to discover the meaning and purpose of your life.

It was a journey of many wild and wonderful adventures, living on the edge and dancing with the shadows.

But you were never alone, you were guided by your own soul.

Yoga and meditation brought peace and a certain level of equilibrium.

But your hunger for the truth was not satisfied, and you set out for India, drawn by an ancient memory of your spiritual roots in that country.

In coming to the ashram, you met Bhagwan and found your spiritual family. This pointed you in the direction of a home inside yourself.

As I sit here, holding hands with you from so long ago, and see how my life unfolded, I can bless the trials and tribulations, the suffering, and the joys experienced on the journey.

Empathy for Others

The pain you experienced as a young girl gave you a deep empathy and an open heart for the pain of others. But you've been hard on yourself, unnecessarily, thinking you could have done so many things differently and better. That is normal for one who lost her mama so young and had to grow up without an adequate reflection of your own goodness and worth. Your mama could have given that to you, but it was not to be.

I hope you can see now that everything happened for a reason; to help you become the person you needed to be. Nothing was wrong. In the grand scheme of things, it was all meant to be.

Your vision and passion for the truth gave birth to work that has changed the lives of many men and women around the world and is still doing so.

I know your heart was broken when you lost your daddy, and in many ways that little girl is still crying for him. But death comes to everyone. It is a natural part of life.

Who knows when or why people die? And thankfully you shared so many good times with your daddy over the years.

I hope you know that the love you shared never leaves you. Even when the form is gone, the spirit of your mama is here with you every day, your daddy is inside you always. This is one thing you can trust.

Devotion to Truth

And here we are, all these years later. How could you have known that you would one day marry a man who would meet you on so many levels, matching your love of adventure and your devotion to the Truth?

Who could have foreseen that together you would create the home and a retreat center on land you love so deeply, nestled in the Blue Ridge Mountains with meadows and forests all around? Making a place for others to come home to themselves and remember who they are. We have called it Samasati Sanctuary: a refuge for the soul.

My darling girl, I love you unconditionally and wholeheartedly. Please let this benediction wash away your tears and any trace of self-doubt. I love you as I love myself. Eternally.

My beloved child, how could you have known all those years ago, that this ragged and rough, mysterious, and miraculous journey was leading you here, to this moment, here and now, where nothing is missing, and everything is fulfilled?

Gautam Buddha said life is suffering. Osho said life is a celebration. It is both and it is ours to live, all of it, fully, as we fumble our way towards freedom and our own awakening.

"Gate, Gate, Param Gate, Parasamgate, Bodhi Swaha!" Oh, what an awakening!

Fumbling towards Freedom / Rajyo Allen

My Teachers

My longing for freedom has taken me to many teachers and wise beings, and I have been blessed to drink from the well of their wisdom to quench my thirst.

My father, Ricky Cunnington, who was my first teacher, and life-long spiritual companion.

My brother, Graham Cunnington, who's wisdom, compassion, and creativity never cease to inspire me.

Bhagwan/ Osho, who inspired me to embrace all aspects of life in one rich tapestry of love, joy, silence, celebration and freedom.

Poonjaji, the Indian sage and disciple of Ramana Maharshi, who I met after Osho died.

Faisel Muqquadim, who taught me the Diamond Logos work.

AH Almaas, who taught me the Enneagram and Essential States.

Leonard Jacobsen, an ordinary man from Australia, who was a teacher of Presence for me.

Eckhart Tolle, with his simple and profound embodiment of the awakened state.

Francis Weller, psychotherapist and author, who helped me integrate my initiatory journey.

Mooji, the Jamaican-English-Rasta guru who reminds me of the simplicity of Being that is our Natural state.

Miranda Macpherson, who transmitted to me the message she received in Ramana's cave on the holy mountain of Arunachala in Southern India: "Be Nothing, Do Nothing, Get Nothing,

Relinquish Nothing, Seek for Nothing. Be as you are. Rest in God."

Mutribo, my spiritual sannyasin friend, who has done the deep work to wake up, and has been a precious guide on my journey home.

Alima, precious friend, devoted seeker. Onwards and inwards we go, always.

To all of you, a deep bow of gratitude.

Manor House / 905-648-4797
www.manor-house-publishing.com